High Agency Human

Other Works by Vickie Lanthier

Best Hikes: Ottawa–Gatineau
Southeastern Ontario Trail Directory

HIGH

Navigate Adversity
and Live BIG

AGENCY

VICKIE M.
LANTHIER

HUMAN

Gibson Quinn Publishing

PERTH

Gibson Quinn Publishing, Perth, K7H 3M6

© 2026 by Vickie M. Lanthier

All rights reserved. No part of this publication may be used or reproduced in any manner whatsoever without the prior written consent of the publisher, except in the case of brief quotations in reviews. For more information, write to Gibson Quinn Publishing at PO Box 20030, Perth, Ontario K7H 3M6.

This publication is sold with the understanding that neither the author nor the publisher is engaged in rendering legal, investment, accounting, or other professional services; nor do they make any representations or warranties with respect to the accuracy or completeness of its contents. The author and publisher disclaim any implied warranties of merchantability or fitness for particular purposes. The advice and strategies contained herein may not be suitable for your situation. You should consult with a professional when appropriate. Neither the publisher nor the author shall be liable for any loss of profit or any other commercial damages, including but not limited to special, incidental, consequential, personal, or other damages.

High Agency Human: Navigate Adversity and Live Big
by Vickie M. Lanthier
Published 2026
Printed in the United States of America
First edition

ISBN: 979-8-89989-068-0 (paperback)
ISBN: 979-8-89989-069-7 (hardcover)
ISBN: 979-8-89989-070-3 (ebook)
ISBN: 979-8-89989-071-0 (audiobook)

Edited by AJ Harper
Copyedited by Zoë Bird
Proofread by KellyAnn Bessa
Designed by Choi Messer
Cover design by Pete Garceau

To you, the capable and driven: You're likely ahead of the game in a lot of ways, yet familiar with the exhaustion and the weight of the consequences that come when life catches us off guard.

This book isn't going to stop hurdles and chaos from happening, but it might just give you an edge.

And an edge is all we need.

CONTENTS

CHAPTER 1
Adversity Isn't Running the Show   1
The best way out is always through.—Robert Frost

CHAPTER 2
Pull the Emergency Brake   17
It's no use saying, "We're doing our best." You have got to succeed in doing what's necessary.—Winston Churchill

CHAPTER 3
Calibrate Your Baseline   37
There is nothing as confining as the prisons of our own perceptions.—William Shakespeare

CHAPTER 4
Master the Mundane   55
Good and evil both increase at compound interest. That is why little decisions you and I make every day are of such infinite importance.—C.S. Lewis

CHAPTER 5
Activate High Agency   73
Man is nothing else but what he makes of himself.
—Jean-Paul Sartre

CHAPTER 6
Boost Protective Buffers   89
Invest in preparedness, not in prediction.
—Nassim Taleb

CHAPTER 7
Pursue Peak Conditioning   113
The purpose of training is to tighten up the slack, toughen the body, and polish the spirit.—Morihei Ueshiba

CHAPTER 8
Switch Off Autopilot   129
You have to assemble your life yourself, action by action.—Marcus Aurelius

CHAPTER 9
High Agency Human   143
Life is like a game of cards. The hand you are dealt is determinism; the way you play it is free will.—Jawaharlal Nehru

Book Club Discussion Questions   153

Big Life Reflective Questions   155

Acknowledgments   159

Notes   161

About the Author   173

DEFINITION

High Agency Human™
/noun/
hi·AY·juhn·see·HYOO·muhn

1: A person who
- Is capable in the face of uncertainty and challenge
- Bends reality to support desired outcomes
- Takes ownership over their actions and the consequences

CHAPTER 1

Adversity Isn't Running the Show

The best way out is always through.
—Robert Frost

Most of us hate the grit and thickness in the air; it's wildly uncomfortable. The haze of desert heat wraps around the mind like a weighted blanket and a strong headwind batters the body. The pocket of discomfort reminds me of our aliveness.

I glance at the long line of troops queueing to get on the stark gray military aircraft for transport back into Afghanistan. They are engaged in a mixture of laughter, intense discussion, and silence. A technician emerges from the aircraft and walks toward me. With the pained effort of a child being forced to apologize when they believe they've done nothing wrong, he announces, "The pilots want me to ask if you'd like to sit in the cockpit with them for the flight." He waits for my response.

HIGH AGENCY HUMAN

"Yeah, all right then," I reply.

A few infantry troops behind me scoff.

"You lucky son of a ..." my buddy Jones[1] says, throwing his hands up in the air. He's a huge plane enthusiast.

The technician frowns. "Follow me, Master Corporal." He leads me past the lineup, onto the aircraft, and up to the cockpit, where two pilots look back at me from their seats with the biggest grins.

I buckle into the bench seat behind them and put on a headset. With the troops now all on board, we take flight. We reach altitude with nothing but blue skies, and the pilots' body language relaxes slightly. I figure this is as good a moment as any to ask a favor.

"Since there are two seats available here, could Jones come up as well?" I ask in my politest, most hopeful voice. "He's interested in planes and would love it. It would make his day."

The pilots' hesitation is immediate. "Well, you know, we're not really supposed to..." one begins.

"What do I need to do to get you guys to say yes?" I ask.

Without missing a beat, one of the pilots replies, "What do you have to offer?"

As I ponder possible responses, the other pilot calls his waypoint in to air traffic control in whatever country we are over now. We are flying a preselected route, and the pilots call in our location at certain intervals.

---

[1] Some names and identifying details of the people described in this book have been altered to protect their privacy.

"All right, gentlemen, I will call out the next waypoint over the radio in my best late-night TV host voice if you allow Jones to come up here for the rest of the flight."

Their faces light up. "You're in. Deal."

The copilot switches seats with me and goes over the radio call signs and what to say. I repeat the sentence over and over in my head. I work in communications and, while it's familiar, air force lingo is slightly different from what I am used to in the army. The pilot nods that it is time to transmit.

I take a breath, press the switch, and speak the rehearsed line with an absurd amount of subtext.

As soon as the transmission ends, the pilots whoop with laughter.

"Right, so can you call the technician to get Jones now?" I ask.

"Yeah, of course. That was brilliant."

The technician fishes Jones from the sea of troops in the back.

"How awesome is this?! And how the hell did you pull it off?" Jones says as he sits beside me on the bench, his eyes as wide as saucers, his smile emitting childlike joy.

I lean back into the seat, pretty darn pleased with myself. We are flying back into austere conditions, rocket attacks, extreme weather, and the deaths of friends. What we are going through—going back into—is what sweetens this moment in the cockpit with Jones. We hold adversity and well-being in the same breath; this is our big life. In these conditions, we radiate aliveness. I'm at the height of my career; doors now open without my even trying, just like today. I am a communications expert, respected leader, skilled freefall parachutist, award recipient, and speaker, and I have multiple deployment experiences. This moment right here, I did this. I created this.

I look out over the pilot's shoulder into the clear blue sky and a full palette of beige terrain staring back at me through the cockpit window. Endless possibilities for the future race in my mind like a herd of wild animals roaming free, knowing they can do so forever.

I wonder what those air traffic controllers thought.

My eyes slowly open to clear blue skies, but not from the cockpit of a plane. And oh, dear God, what is that smell? It's the same offending odor you pick up walking by a teenager's room when they keep their door shut too often and swear they showered but didn't. Except I'm not a teenager and this isn't a room. The stench fogs the car windows. I need to stop passing out in parking lots. I look down at my cheap Walmart watch and 5:16 a.m. blinks back. Do I need to work or go to school today? Both? Definitely both. But more importantly, what's due today? I can't remember. *Where's that agenda?*

I start rifling through the old army duffel in the backseat. It's been years since that flight into Afghanistan. While adversity is still ever-present as I try to make it through nursing school and life after the military, well-being has dropped off my radar. This is no longer a big life. My aliveness has dimmed into a distant, foreign memory. One sock, two socks—ah, there it is, deodorant. First win of the day. Glancing out into the parking lot, I make sure no one is around before I quickly change. The paper agenda sits on the front seat, silently mocking my efforts to endure with its many highlights, underlines, and circled words. A sense of overwhelm threatens my ability to remain calm. Sad how there are no line items for me. *Shit, shit, shit.* I forgot to submit my time sheet for work yesterday, and there's an essay due today that I haven't even started yet. *It's fine. I'm fine. Everything is fine.*

My cell phone beeps with a new email. *No thank you.* I throw it on the passenger seat and start the car. If I hustle, I can sneak into the gym showers at work. They will be clean and empty at this hour.

Last night was the second I've spent in my car. I'm not homeless, just exhausted. Making the drive back to my little apartment forty minutes from the city isn't always the safest option after a fourteen- or sixteen-hour day.

I'm pretty sure there are work clothes in this rust bucket somewhere. I can clock a few hours, race to class, call the bank on my break, jump back to work, then return to school and stay until 10:00 p.m.

A third night in the car is a distinct possibility.

I did this. I created this.

HIGH AGENCY HUMAN

A glance down at my phone reveals the screen saver, a photograph of me and Jones in that cockpit. It is a sobering reminder that even in the thick of it, adversity and well-being can coexist. Hell, hard moments can even lead to greater well-being and opportunity.

I learned this lesson at the age of nineteen, after a life-altering event I experienced on my first military contract. It started with a routine task on a sunny day and quickly escalated into a shitstorm that cost me my front teeth.

"Corporal," barked the troop warrant officer from across the compound. I lifted my head to see him beelining right for me. "You'll crew-command so the driver can take the bison out for a spin." ("The bison" was an armored personnel carrier we used as a communications vehicle.)

"But I don't have a helmet," I said.

The troop warrant officer rolled his eyes. "It's just on base, no need."

"But I don't know how to crew-command?!"

"Jesus, Lanthier, it's easy," he said. "Just say 'clear right, clear left' when you get to intersections." Then he walked away.

My gut churned with the instinct that this would be a whole lot of bad news bears, but I climbed up into the crew commander's hatch just the same. I mean, it was just a spin on paved roads, so no big deal, right?

First intersection. "Clear left, clear right," I said into the headset.

The driver responded and we proceeded. *This isn't so bad*, I thought. I felt important to be crew-commanding, too, even though I'd never admit that out loud and risk seeming uncool.

We came up to the next intersection, then the next, driving further away from the troop lines. The driver, Brown, decided to swing off the paved roads and into the training area.

"We're heading back soon, right?" I asked.

"In a minute. Let's really test it!" Brown replied. He was a regular force soldier and I was a reservist, so I figured he knew better. He started speeding through the training field, which was nothing but dirt, grass, and uneven terrain. With each bump, my heart sank a little more.

We approached "Five Fingers," a set of dunes used for training and testing vehicles or, if our bosses were feeling spicy, hills from hell that we ran up and down repeatedly for morning fitness drills.

Brown took the vehicle right up the steep dune tracks. I was standing on a cushioned seat with my body half out of the cupola, a hatched opening above the main body of the tank, to crew-command. We reached the top, tilted forward, and then went down far too damn fast, hitting a tank ditch and crashing back onto the ground with a thunderous thump. Dust from the impact engulfed us. I wasn't wearing a helmet or a seat belt. This is how people die in training accidents.

I took the cupola through the chin, knocking out four whole teeth, fracturing my upper jaw, breaking my nose, and cracking several ribs.

Tapping Brown on the shoulder, I attempted to say, "Hospital."

Brown turned around to see me covered in red and started driving toward the base hospital while I took off my blood-soaked combat shirt, went back up to retrieve my teeth, started first aid, and pulled out my military and health card. Time moved slowly and with clarity.

When the vehicle stopped, I climbed out of the hatch myself, moving to the front of the tank. Then the shock wore off and I started to cry, mumbling that I couldn't take the last step down. Brown came over, whisked me into his arms, walked towards the hospital entrance, and kicked open the double doors with his foot. The hallways were empty and eerily quiet.

"Medic!" he yelled, his voice trembling.

A rush of medics, nurses, and doctors flooded the hall. They didn't hide their looks of shock as orders were given. This was a scene straight out of the movies.

AFTER TWO DAYS OFF FOR surgeries, I showed up for morning physical fitness with black eyes, cotton up my nose with black sutures sticking out like a bull's ring, and no top front teeth.

It was an obstacle course day. The warrant officer looked at me like I was insane. "What the hell, Lanthier? No way. Go home."

I pulled out my med chit defiantly. "Nowhere on here does it say I can't." Out of all the restrictions the doctors had listed, not one stated that I couldn't run alongside the rest of the platoon.

"I won't climb a single obstacle," I promised.

It would have been understandable if I hadn't participated in fitness. It would have been understandable if I had taken a few days of rest to recover. It would have been understandable if I had cut the contract and gone home. Any of those options would have been okay.

At that moment, however, a simple question crossed my mind: *What's the most courageous thing I can do right now? If I don't "make it" here, on my first contract, then I have nowhere to go.* I was scared, but I sure as hell wasn't going back to small-town life. There had to be more. I had to be more.

The warrant officer begrudgingly agreed to let me participate.

After physical training, I dressed in jean overalls and a pale-yellow tee and headed over for breakfast. News of the accident had already spread through the base faster than a church phone tree. My face bruised and stitched, I walked into the mess hall and gave a small nod to the cooks, who passed me a smoothie. The old airborne soldiers already sitting down mid-meal stared at me, mouths agape.

THE NATURE OF ADVERSITY

THE DECISION TO JOIN PHYSICAL training that morning changed the course of my life, a sliding door moment with ripple effects I still feel today. Though it was actually fear-based, my response to adversity was seen as admirable. Because of it, I developed a reputation for working hard and through obstacles, was chosen for military deployments and jobs, and gained respect from the right people. Most importantly, the realization set in that through our responses, we influence our outcomes.

Adversity isn't running the show. You are.

It's not the partner, the job, or world events. It's not the million little cuts riddling our lives. It's us. We're running the show.

Life is hard. We are all doing our best and it is still hard. You can be the fittest human on the planet and eat boatloads of greens your whole life only to face disease. Or the most supportive parent who does everything for your family and is still drowning financially. Or the community cheerleader, the one who shows up to every event, yet struggles with loneliness. You can be all the things and adversity will still come knocking.

In this book, "adversity" encompasses acute and chronic hardships. We might use words like *struggle, challenge, overwhelm,* or even *trauma* and *crisis* to describe it. Adversity can include financial setbacks, health challenges, natural disasters or man-made hardships, and the deaths of loved ones.

Sometimes we can't catch a break, or it seems like we've been cursed with a string of bad luck. Our challenges can feel like gut punches or a multitude of little cuts over time. We let them fester and weigh down our lives to our detriment, though. When we take control, we choose which sliding door to walk through. We create an opportunity to thrive.

Some of us try to pretend that everything is fine by keeping up appearances and doubling down on our efforts to maintain the status quo. Others freeze up like fainting goats.

Or, if you're like me and too proud to admit when you're in over your head, you deploy gum and duct tape everywhere and just pray that it'll hold.

Adverse events are part and parcel of living a big life, and we need to learn to live with and move through them. Adversity rules our lives when we can't see past it, when we passively allow life to happen to us. It's easy to unconsciously submit to adversity's chaotic tempo and truck along to the jerky cadence it sets for us. It's also up to us to see that there is a way through, a path ahead, and a means to prepare for hard times.

IT STARTS WITH AGENCY

I CLICK MY PHONE OFF again and the picture of my confident past self disappears into blackness. *Can I get through this mess I'm in now?* Today would indicate otherwise. It's shit. An overdue bill notice has come in the mail, I got

HIGH AGENCY HUMAN

a parking ticket this morning, and I'm not sure what I can afford for lunch. The mental math distracts me from the class I'm in—but then the sense of urgency in the air knocks me out of my worried daydream.

Four students are trying desperately to run a simulation without messing up, a mock emergency in which they attempt to save a dummy's life as monitors beep incessantly and the fluorescent lighting flickers overhead. The group's student leader stutters commands and stumbles to maintain control as the fake patient continues to tank. I see the student leader glance down and then over at her peers, including me. Her hesitation feels like an invitation.

I place my hand gently on her shoulder and take over. The sequence runs imperfectly, but in a controlled fashion.

"End scenario. All right, let's go over what just happened," the instructor says.

It's lab day, and instead of practicing giving injections or calculating medications, we are running code drills. The scenarios are a few minutes each, just long enough for us to get a sense of different emergency events.

I stand off to the side again, ready to listen. As the professor starts going over the learning points in the scenario, I'm nudged gently in the ribs.

Matt, a friend and fellow student, leans in and whispers, "This is the first time I've seen you smile in the whole damn program."

He's right: It's the first time I've felt good in ages. I run my hand over the scar on my chin, a remnant of the tank accident. Once prominent, it is now faded, much like the lessons it originally provided. *Why on earth am I sleeping in my car, wearing myself out, and struggling with finances? I don't need to be here.* I am no longer listening to the professor but lost in the realization that I can choose how to face the struggles in front of me. I make a mental note to mull over what needs to change on our next break.

Having high agency means possessing both the belief and the capacity to influence outcomes. It is your intrinsic sense of control and ability to take ownership of your responses, decisions, and actions instead of letting them be dictated solely by external events or forces.

While most accept this broad definition, academics can't quite agree on the specific components of agency. Some say they are intentionality, forethought, self-reactiveness—motivating and regulating one's own actions—and self-reflectiveness, core features of agency as developed by psychologist Albert Bandura, while others include confidence, competence, and the desire to achieve. Personal agency is a concept closely linked with free will and self-efficacy. It includes both mindset and action.

Think of personal agency as a spectrum, not an inherent trait we are born with but a mindset that can either atrophy or be cultivated. A low agency mindset tends to be reactive and less questioning. A high agency person tends to be active, resourceful, and biased toward action. They find or create ways to achieve goals. The classic example is that people with a low agency mindset see life as happening to them, while people with a high agency mindset believe that they are happening to life.

There can be areas where or seasons of life when you operate in lower or higher agency. In Afghanistan, I was happening to life and thriving. No matter what was thrown our way, I felt capable and in control of my own outcomes. Experiences became stepping stones to reach the next goal. At university, life happened to me. I was a passive participant who allowed adversity to run the show. In Afghanistan, I exercised high agency; in university, low agency. Thankfully—as you will discover—the spectrum of low to high agency can be influenced.

We'll move forward with the understanding that high agency is a state where you feel a sense of control over and in life while actively and effectively participating in your own outcomes. The characteristics of High Agency Humans combine powerfully to help them navigate the hardships that adversity brings.

The questions I am asked most often are:

- How did you pivot so fast?
- How can you afford so many vacations?
- How do you have so much free time?
- How are you always ready for (nearly) anything?

This book is a response to those questions, a collection of what I've experienced, put into practice, and continue to learn along the way. That said, you don't have to implement every thought and framework in this book to benefit. By the time you read the final page, you will realize that you can live well no matter what adversity comes your way.

Operating in a high agency state, you can manage what is in front of you and prepare for the next challenge. It's your mindset that determines your next step, and that step that carves your path. Remember: *Adversity isn't running the show. You are.*

CHAPTER 2

Pull the Emergency Brake

It's no use saying, "We're doing our best."
You have got to succeed in doing what's necessary.
—Winston Churchill

ONE MINUTE IT WAS BLUE skies and sunshine—the next, an imposing cloud appeared over the mountain a half-mile away and covered its jagged gray peaks and impressive glaciers in darkness.

My friend Marlena and I were hiking the Iceline Trail in Yoho National Park in the Canadian Rockies, a trail filled with glaciers, bright turquoise lakes, and incredible views of the valley below. We had broken free of the tree line and hiked past some scree when the cloud emerged. Hikers on the trail below us turned back, but we opted to stay after checking the weather satellite map. It was just a blip in the day. We put on our Gore-Tex gear, huddled under the emergency blanket, and broke out some snacks.

HIGH AGENCY HUMAN

Perfectly safe and happy, we watched Mother Nature's show in awe. The sky pitched hail for perhaps a minute or two while the sun lit the other side of the valley in front of us, turning its bright greens and lush waterfalls radiant. As we leaned against the cold, harsh rocks, I felt at peace. Once the weather passed, we continued on what turned out to be one of my favorite trails and hikes to date.

Have you ever been to the mountains? If so, do you remember the first time you hiked up to a high point and looked around at the landscape? It is breathtaking in the true sense of the word. Because I live in Ontario, it's normal for my friends and family to vacation in the Canadian Rockies. Nearly everyone, including me, comes home to immediately profess out loud that they are now a mountain person.

Mountains have a way of making us feel humbled, connected, and aligned. Once back home amidst the chaos, we feel driven to figure out how we can make the move west and forever keep that high of being amongst giants. Some do move, while the rest of us keep dreaming about it. What is it about mountains that obsesses us so completely we can't see past them?

With the array of experiences that come with military deployments, one would think that soldiers would be insane to say they want to go back; yet that's exactly how many of them feel. Veterans are often released only to bounce right back to overseas contracts. What is it about deployments that have soldiers and veterans running back like horses to a barn fire?

One aspect of serving on military deployments is the same as being in the mountains: in both instances, our scope of concern is narrowed to our immediate needs and situation. This reduction is accompanied by a sense of agency and freedom.

Hiking in the mountains requires that we focus on navigation and our physical state and surroundings. We check in on fellow hikers and watch for potential threats like wildlife, weather, and terrain. We're in the now and little else matters. The weight of the world has lifted.

It can be the same on military deployments, which require operational awareness and taking care of our physical state and mental well-being. We check in on our teammates and watch for potential threats like others, weather, and terrain. We're in the now and little else matters. The weight of the world has lifted. Life is simplified—not easy, mind you, but simplified, reduced to the most basic needs. This can create a sense of relief so deep it is almost euphoric.

No fights with the in-laws or constant pings from work. No emails to check. Little to no cell reception. Life isn't scheduled in five-minute increments, and I don't care that John got promoted before me at work or that the neighbor hasn't cut their lawn in weeks.

In both the mountains and on deployment, we are brought back to foundational needs. Perhaps there is

HIGH AGENCY HUMAN

something to those moments that we can apply in everyday life.

Over the years, in the face of adversity, I imposed this state of reduction on myself in order to find my footing again. This act has been instinctual in nature, and yet—as with most things in life—our ideas and actions are rarely unique. The deeper I dove, the more I discovered similar or supporting theories and frameworks that strategically strip life down to its essentials to help people endure and navigate through adversity. In his book *Essentialism*, author Greg McKeown writes about eliminating the nonessential to focus on what truly matters, especially during high-stress periods. Resilience researcher Ann Masten highlights our need to know our limits and pull back to the basics to survive prolonged adversity. Otherwise, we risk reaching "surge capacity," the term Masten uses to describe the upper limit of our ability to use the adaptive systems best suited for short-term survival over long-term stress. The Adaptive Calibration Model by Ellis, Shirtcliff, and Del Giudice describes how humans adjust effort and energy use based on perceived stress or threat. This biological model recognizes that pulling back is an adaptive, not weak, response.

The scope of a reduction can be as wide or narrow as we need it to be, a pull on the emergency brake that reminds us we all can create and have control over our future. This chapter shows you how to hit pause when life speeds up and create space for agency to return.

You catch a break by creating one.

DO (SIGNIFICANTLY) LESS TO DO (SIGNIFICANTLY) BETTER

SIMPLIFY TO AMPLIFY IS THE mantra that entrepreneur powerhouse and author Marie Forleo has reiterated time and again in her interviews and articles. As she says, "Simplifying is almost always the answer if you want to decrease stress and fatigue while increasing results." Simplification gives us the much-needed space to move forward. Yet, as author Leidy Klotz clearly illustrates in his book *Subtract: The Untapped Science of Less*, subtraction is not our go-to response to problems. Normally, our default reaction is to add. If you're looking to create the break you need, start with clearing the path by doing less.

The outcome of a reduction is akin to the "fresh start effect": a gateway to a new path, one that deviates from the one we were previously on. The fresh start effect comes through change we go into feeling motivated and hopeful of success. It's the New Year, the start of a fresh semester, or the first day of a new job. It's moving to a new town, cracking open a new notepad, or planning the layout of a new home.

According to behavioral science researchers Dai, Milkman, and Riis, the fresh start effect works for some and not for others. If you already have a successful, steady routine, a fresh start can be disruptive. For others, it's a chance to realign or "finally get it right." The thing is that the fresh start effect isn't a standalone solution. You need other tools to elicit change.

Although both the fresh start effect and a reduction can offer opportunities to realign with your values, the main differences between the two are in the catalyst, level of motivation, and length of time you need to keep them in play.

Reductions respond to adversities and bring the benefits of being in the mountains home. They are a narrowing of focus to the fundamentals, a catapult into action to deal with an immediate need. A reduction is a kind of surge, but instead of doing more, you do less. And, as I mentioned, you do less better. Doing less might feel like quitting—if you think of it that way—but know that quitting can be act of resiliency. A reduction also gives you breathing room, after the immediate response, to create the foundation you need to withstand future adversities.

DIGGING OUT OF REAL-LIFE RUTS

A YEAR AFTER SLEEPING IN the car, my tempo hasn't waned. I have a beautiful condo in the city that's enough to make it seem, at least to the outside world, like I'm doing well. I am not. I am more than $80,000 in debt and every dollar weighs me down. I stare at my bank balances online; there's no way to hide from it, I don't have enough to pay the mortgage. Again. I'm a hundred dollars shy and my payment is due tomorrow.

A rush of shame overwhelms me. *How am I getting myself out of this?* I called Veterans Affairs for help yesterday but was too proud to continue with the process. Those services should be for veterans who really need help, not sorry saps who put themselves in a pickle.[2] I also tried talking to the bank about debt consolidation this morning, and they flat-out refused after looking at my accounts. Then I called the mortgage company to remortgage and absorb the debt, and they also refused. I pick up the phone and dial a friend.

"I'm sorry... hate asking... tried everything..." I say between waves of tears and humiliation.

"Are you okay?" Sam asks.

"I am, just in a tough spot at the moment." I am beside myself about asking a friend for money. It is gutting, but I'm desperate. I'll figure out the rest later. "I can pay you back on Tuesday when I send more clothes to the consignment store, I promise."

Sam calmly responds, "It's okay, honestly. Hey, what's your email? I'll send a transfer."

"Thank you, I owe you," I say before hanging up.

Wiping away tears and ego, I get online to transfer the funds and pay my mortgage. Sam didn't send a hundred dollars; he sent a thousand, with a note stating that I don't need to pay him back. My body instantly slumps against the wall in relief, then relaxes into a puddle of gratitude.

While Sam helped with a quick fix by sending funds, the long-term solution is up to me. Instead of the usual

---

[2] A bit of misplaced ego here. I could and perhaps should have taken advantage of the services offered by Veterans Affairs Canada. If you need help, please reach out to your local services and organizations for it.

whys, I start contemplating the hows and whats. *How can I earn more and reduce debt? What can I do right now? What can I take off my plate?*

The best way to pay Sam back is to do well and get out of this. Finding my footing means implementing an immediate and radical reduction.

IMPLEMENTING A REDUCTION

A REDUCTION PERMITS YOU TO go back to basics, regardless of what the outside world thinks. It helps you put yourself and your future first and provides a reset, a clean slate from which you can open up to possibilities.

The fundamentals are derived from Maslow's hierarchy of needs. In 1943, Abraham Maslow introduced his popular psychological theory in his book *A Theory of Human Motivation*.[3] The model is in the shape of a pyramid, with five levels that represent our needs in order of priority. At the base is physiological needs, followed by safety needs, love and belonging, esteem, and self-actualization as the peak of the triangle.

Back in my condo, I scribble a self-check derived from Maslow's hierarchy of needs and carefully consider each one. The results are a clear indication that yes, my physiological needs—like food, shelter, and warmth—are threatened

---

[3] Further research indicates that Maslow "borrowed heavily" from the beliefs of the Blackfoot Nation (Siksika) in Canada after a visit to the First Nations community.

but so far being met. And yes, being in good physical health and having stable finances—under safety—are the biggest needs going unmet. The rest, well, it can wait.

I start by taking a very stoic approach to brainstorming, recognizing and then pushing aside any emotion to focus on the task at hand. I run around the house and ruthlessly gather items, creating a glorious pile of furniture, clothes, books, and electronics in the middle of the living room. This alone feels like a triumph. Within a few hours, I have taken pictures and placed for-sale ads on social media, washed and prepped clothes for the consignment store, and canceled all my well-intentioned-yet-never-used workout and streaming service subscriptions. This first round of effort generates enough to address my immediate financial needs.

My beautiful, modern condo has vaulted ceilings and a gorgeous view of treetops off the balcony. The reality is that, even though the equity has gone up nicely, I have too much debt to remortgage. But I could sell it. Before I have a chance to reconsider, I call the realtor and list it. Three days later, it sells.

With the sale, I clear my debt and have a little left over to make a down payment on a new home build in the country which is set to be finished in just over a year. That will still leave me homeless for a while. I swallow my pride and decide to move into my mother's basement.

It's not that I loved being a grown-ass adult moving back in with a parent, it's that it made the most sense and the option, thankfully, was available. Sometimes you have to make a few moves that ding your pride (and dating life) so you can find your footing again. Instead of letting ego and fear get in the way, you have to own the decisions that are right for you. I remember my mother once saying, "If you can own it, then others can't pick on you." I can reframe living with my mother in adulthood so that I'm proud to have such a close, supportive relationship with her. Although not everyone has the support system in place to make such a move, it is important to factor in all possible moves, regardless of how you feel about them, so that the big picture of possibility is clear.

Much like experiencing a storm in the mountains or being on a military deployment, we can narrow our focus to move through hard times. The application of a reduction to my finances wasn't just budgeting and paying down debt, it was building breathing room. The liberating realization is that reduction can also be used to alleviate compounding stressors before relationships, finances, or health worsen.

Here's how we break down a reduction.

1.

First, we create space by permitting ourselves to narrow our focus to fundamental needs and respond to the event only. Just as with the financial hurdle I went through, we start with a self-check against the bottom two tiers of Maslow's hierarchy: physiological and safety needs.

2.

The second step is to eliminate everything beyond those needs. Life is different right now, and we need to adjust our expectations. We can give ourselves permission to cancel everything except what is absolutely necessary to meet our physiological and safety needs, and be ruthless about it. We no longer need to show up for that family gathering or social event. We can toss the old ideology of keeping up with the Joneses out the window and sell whatever we need to stay afloat. It's time to rip up that book of self-imposed rules.

While I was writing this book, my neighbor's ten-year-old spent a day at my place to focus on her art. We spent hours sketching, and partway through, I changed the style of the lion I was working on.

"I'm not following the rules," I said to her as I adjusted the lion's mane.

Without skipping a beat or looking up, she said, "Who says there are any rules?"

I nodded and carried on. The kid reminded me that sometimes we restrict ourselves without realizing it. Adversity often imposes the same threat: Forgetting that we can run the show, we constrain ourselves with false rules.

3.

The next step is to look at how you can address those foundational needs. Write down all the possibilities, even if you think they aren't options for you. It does take some humility to match a need with all possible avenues, many of which may require asking for help from friends, family, or organizations.

4.

The last step is to make it happen and stay in that reduced state until your foundation is solid once again. With my finances, this meant canceling subscriptions, renegotiating plans, talking with the bank, looking at my mortgage, applying to aid programs, selling whatever wasn't an absolute need or of sentimental value (even if it was at a loss), selling my home, and moving in with family for eighteen months.

Amid financial crisis, implementing a reduction meant that I was able to stop my debt from growing, clear existing debt, create an emergency fund, and purchase a new home. I was able to build a base and increase resilience. What I realized while going through this reduction is that you don't have to keep up with the imaginary at the cost of surviving the real.

APPLYING REDUCTION TO OTHER AREAS

FINANCE WAS AN EASY EXAMPLE to help run through the steps of a reduction. The truth is that you can apply this to most areas beyond finance, including your health, relationships, environment, work, side hustle, schedule, or social media.

When our health declines or takes a hit, as I mentioned earlier, our tendency is to add things like new supplements, therapies, and nutritional protocols. But what about doing a self-check against our foundational needs, implementing a reduction, and mastering the basics to gift ourselves the best possible platform from which to heal?

Forget green juice or the latest protein supplement for just a moment and start with basic physiological needs. Are you getting enough quality, consistent sleep? Are you getting outside into the daylight and moving? What about nutrition and connection through community?

Overwhelm, in my book, is also adversity. Or at least, it can lead to adverse events like health issues or unintentional incidents due to an altered health state. The more demands we fill our lives with, the less room we have to live.

As a list person, this is perhaps one of my favorite things to do: Start with a blank calendar. Add only the events and commitments that directly impact your foundational needs. This can include work, medical appointments, etc. Nothing else. Not the social events or volunteer gigs or the long list of shoulds.

The next step is to cluster the appointments and errands. Instead of having your car tune-up, dental checkup, and errands spread throughout the month, see which appointments you can reasonably make for the same day. This is easier to do with appointments you can book months in advance. As for the outliers, leave them off the calendar and cancel them. It's a bold move—but give yourself permission to protect your own downtime. Unless it is a global emergency or a state of war, you don't need to volunteer or show up to events at the expense of your well-being. This sounds dramatic, but you get the idea.

Side hustles are great until they aren't. If you have one and it's starting to feel like a runaway train that's costing you your health, relationships, or peace of mind, it might be time for a reduction. Ask yourself if you *need* to write a book, start a podcast, run workshops, give talks, and be on all the social media platforms. Give yourself permission to master one product, one content type, and one service. Then, if there is room, add—but intentionally. You are in control.

REDUCTION OF BURNOUT

"What happened to you?" Amy, a fellow student said as she waved a finger up and down at my body and blew her cheeks out like a blowfish. As if living in my mother's basement wasn't humiliating enough. *Why, God, why?*

I ignored Amy's question and left as quickly as possible.

I had started drinking coffee and taking caffeine supplements to stay awake enough to drive between home, work, and school, but often it wasn't enough. Even though I no longer slept the occasional night or three in the car, I did nap in parking lots and watch anatomy videos in the car. I was never home long enough to make lunch. My grades were mediocre at best, and my body was falling apart with more determination than my fourteen-year-old car.

Amy was right, I had blown up like a blowfish. With the weight gain, incredible fatigue, and frequent crying, I could no longer recognize the person in the mirror.

Other symptoms arose in the form of nightmares, night sweats, insomnia, severe joint pain, acne, brain fog, hypoglycemia, blurry vision, muscle exhaustion, frequent infections and colds, dizziness, trouble concentrating, abdominal pain, loss of motivation, depression, infrequent menstruation, "pins and needles" in extremities and poor circulation, frequent chills, dry skin, lower back pain, salt cravings, dark circles around the eyes, and extreme mood fluctuations. It was time for the follow-up appointment that the university medical clinic had requested.

The university doctor showed me my lab results and I noted the tanked cortisol, among other factors. I had thought life was unraveling, but it was just me. I was unraveling.

"Congratulations," the doctor said. "You are officially burnt out."

I had already applied a reduction to my finances and somehow missed applying the same method to my health. Instead, I had tried a million different quick fixes in desperation, because who has time to slow down? From restrictive diets to healers to tinctures, I wasted an absurd amount of money on shiny treatments, therapies, and supplements, and it is embarrassing to think back on. I didn't want to take the long road of turning things around by being, well, an adult who respects themselves enough to master some fundamentals. I forgot the golden rule: When they are in conflict, do the things that are good for you over the things you feel like doing. Feelings are often shit navigators.

Now was the time to take a more engaged approach. If I didn't, my body would eventually shut me down, effectively flushing my opportunity to finish the nursing degree and my optimal long-term health down the tubes.

Dr. Gabor Maté describes how stress can become illness in his book *When the Body Says No*. "Stress is a complicated cascade of physical and biochemical responses to powerful emotional stimuli. Physiologically, emotions are themselves electrical, chemical, and hormonal discharges of the human nervous system." No thank you.

In this case, reduction looked like seeking professional help from a physician and an endocrinologist. I focused on sleep first, cleaning out the bedroom, using blackout curtains, and sticking to a bedtime instead of pulling late-night study sessions. Then I tackled nutrition, removing the extra caffeine from my diet and focusing on simple meals of whole foods. Not the coffee, though—for the love of all that is holy, never will I remove the coffee. I took running off my plate and replaced it with five-minute meditations. Finally, I made the harder decision to reduce my academic load to part time.

No longer boxed in by burnout after applying a reduction, I had enough room to take a closer look at what I could do to keep improving my situation.

IT DOESN'T HAVE TO BE A BIG LEAP

Sometimes a reduction is more like a smooth transition, a smaller adjustment in response to misalignment. As a mountain guide and photographer, my friend Nate has a large audience on social media. His pictures of mountain landscapes and cheeky pikas leave us all in a state of awe and wonder. By all measures, he is a successful photographer, adventurer, and social media influencer. A few years ago, he released a video stating that he had ceased his sponsorship deals, sold his expensive camera equipment, and decided to step back from social media. The reason was one I think most social media influencers can relate to: Nate's love of the outdoors was hindered by the perceived pressure to produce incredible photography on each outing. He had no room to simply be present and enjoy nature. Not to mention the toll that hiking with heavy camera gear was taking on his body and mindset.

"I just want to hike for myself," he messaged me.

The funny thing is, Nate started making changes even earlier and the majority of us who follow his social media account didn't even notice. He was taking pictures with a normal camera and posting on social media once a month versus once a day. I was unaware that he had changed anything because his pictures looked great and he is still out there adventuring every chance he gets.

I messaged him back: "Your 'step back' is really just a shift back to what feels good, back to values instead of letting make-believe pressure dictate your actions. It's like you're taking your autonomy back from social media."

"Love all that! That's exactly it," Nate replied.

WHEN OTHERS (OR YOU) DOUBT YOUR ACTIONS

You'll likely experience a degree of hesitation along the way, in others or yourself. When my own hesitation arises, it comes in the form of fear of being judged by others for not adhering to societal expectations at the cost of my finances, health, and well-being. I try to think back to what my mother said about "owning it." Don't fear that a reduction will set you back or put you off track; instead, focus on how it will give you the space to strengthen your foundation so that you can move toward goals faster and more easily. Despite our very normal reservations, we are all capable of getting ahead by narrowing down with a reduction.

When others doubt you, it can be hard to hold your ground. In 2010, after coming home from my fourth and final deployment, I submitted a request to leave the military.

I was dealing with insomnia and night terrors. Medical staff prescribed antidepressants and sleeping pills to no avail. Change was needed if I was to take control over adversity once more.

In the months that followed, while I waited for the release date to arrive, I walked away from friendships, changed my finances, and gave away most of my possessions. Just as a clean and organized room left me happy, calm, and feeling in control of myself and my environment as a kid, so did reductions as an adult.

This massive reduction of stuff, people, and the military environment left only the fundamentals and a world of possibility to focus on. It was the largest reduction of all. Leaving the military, and the actions I was taking prior to release, were such a change that a coworker asked if I was planning to commit suicide. They joked that I wouldn't last a year and civilian life was too big a shift. Friends thought that I wasn't thinking things through, because who on earth would walk away from a government pension? What they didn't realize is that I didn't see it as giving up but moving on.

When you take control, people might react badly or seem unsupportive—and that's okay. While some may question, others may surprise you by stepping up to support and encourage you through your reduction. Hold firm, knowing that while it may seem unconventional, you are putting your best interests first.

HIGH AGENCY HUMAN

FIRST STEP IN THE LONG GAME

PULLING THE EMERGENCY BRAKE WITH a reduction stops the current trajectory and can give you the space you need to redirect your efforts and influence outcomes. You don't have to quit your job or sell your house. As you saw with Nate, a reduction can be a small action with big impact. Acting on this level is a ritual of self-respect, a show of appreciation for your future. The effects of a reduction will not ripple sustainably, though, unless you take a look inward to resolve that space and prevent the reemergence of the same weight you felt in the initial situation. Which means that, to begin building up to a big life, we'll work on calibrating perspectives in the next chapter.

CHAPTER 3

Calibrate Your Baseline

There is nothing as confining as the prisons of our own perceptions.
—William Shakespeare

THREE GUNSHOTS RANG OUT IN the air. Instead of reaching their intended target, the bullets tore through the body of a bright, energetic young professional who, until this moment, was having an average day during an average week in an average but good life. At the age of twenty-three, Brandon Peacock was now bleeding out on the barbershop floor.

Brandon could easily have missed this moment. He had decided to get a haircut after work and left earlier than usual, then stopped to get gas on the way even though the tank was half full and he normally let it go to near empty. Each moment compounded so that he arrived at an exact, life-altering moment.

Brandon was walking along the sidewalk, nearing the barber shop, when the first shot was fired. He instinctively rushed into the shop for cover with the owner's wife urging him in toward safety.

One shot.

Two shots.

Three shots.

His body shielded her from each.

Just as a few decisions led to Brandon being there for this event, specific actions happened at just the right time for him to survive. The shop owner's wife saved his life by quickly reacting and grabbing fresh towels to stanch his wounds. She pressed her body weight to the most critical wound first; Brandon was hit in the femoral artery and rapidly losing blood with each heartbeat. They called 911. Ottawa Police were able to respond within four minutes. The first officer on the scene quickly applied a tourniquet.

The shop owner's wife later told Brandon that she was certain he was about to die in front of her. Death, however, wasn't on his mind. While he lay there on the shop floor, he asked himself one simple yet powerful question: *Am I proud of the legacy I'll leave behind?*

His answer was a resounding no.

In our interview, Brandon explained, "That [question] was my dying thought at twenty-three. Everybody just assumes you have this montage of your life and all your big events, and I've done some cool stuff at that point, right? I had a great life compared to a lot of people. But I realized I wasn't proud of it because I didn't really make that much of an impact. I was able to do some cool stuff for myself,

I had good friends and good family, but I hadn't made an impact on a larger scale to leave something behind that I was truly proud of."

That question, on that day, was the beginning of Brandon's second life; a still good but no longer average life, one that he wasted no time establishing because he intuitively knew what takes some of us years to realize: Adversity creates an incredible opportunity to participate in our own life outcomes. Depending on our mindset and reaction, an adverse event can act as a defibrillator. Brandon was living the linear corporate path that never felt quite right to him. The event changed how he looked at the world, his place in it, and the future he could create. In that regard, it's a good thing that adversity comes for us all. It can facilitate the perspective shift that drives us forward.

Changes in the way we see the world can come from major disruptions, like the drive-by-shooting Brandon experienced, or from simply being curious and open to conversation and learning. We can adopt new mindsets to create a baseline that benefits us. This kind of growth is worth the acute discomfort of change.

With that, we'll dive right into some perspectives to try on when it comes to dealing with adversity.

ADVERSITY IS NORMAL

WE ACT AS IF ADVERSITY is abnormal, like it is surprising, even shocking: the sudden job loss, natural disaster, market crash, death of a loved one, or even loss of infrastructure we depend on, like electricity. A moment like this can be difficult, uncomfortable, and intimidating. It's an affront to our ideal, steady state. *How dare life do this to me?*

Except, as we adopt a High Agency Human mindset, we embrace that life isn't happening to us, but us to life. While we can't always anticipate the type of difficulty we'll encounter, the fact that we will be challenged should be a known and accepted component of life's trajectory. There is no path ahead where you can live a full existence and completely avoid hardship. Life is mutable, no matter how much we insist it be otherwise.

Our experiences are cyclic, with high times and hurdles. You can flip through history books or dive into nature to find these patterns everywhere. Take the phenomenon of secondary succession, for example, a part of the foundational concept of ecological succession. It occurs in different terrains and over varied timelines. Secondary succession is nature's way of adapting and regenerating after disruptions such as the classic examples of forest fires and volcanic eruptions. After an event, the pioneer species, the first species to repopulate the barren terrain after a disturbance, springs to new life. After a few years, the environment recovers further with the growth of intermediate species like shrubs and young trees—secondary succession. As the plants mature, they become a climax community and reestablish the environment. These communities continue to mature until the next disruption, adjusting their species composition along the way in response to smaller changes like resource availability, and then the cycle begins once more. This cycle varies in time and disruption type, but what we do know is that disruptions happen and nature's reaction is secondary succession. It is a pattern of growth, disruption, and resilience.

When you take a closer look at humans instead of plant life, you'll observe that adversity and our navigation through it are just as common. Look at your last ten years and you'll likely notice cyclic ups and downs as well as personal growth and adaptation along the way. Reflect on the hurdles you have endured, like failed relationships, health diagnoses, professional setbacks, vehicle accidents, and extreme weather events. Think of the highs, too, like academic achievements, promotions, thriving relationships, personal growth, serendipitous moments, and unexpected wins.

Adversity is so normal that the average adult experiences thirty-six major life disruptions and 70 percent of adults experience at least one traumatic event in their lifetime. Financially, we see that economic recessions happen every six to eight years and the last five prior to 2025 lasted an average of 10.4 months. Nature tests us as well; in the first six months of 2023, the Federal Emergency Management Agency (FEMA) reported fifty-seven state and county-level disaster declarations and provided $212.1 million in grants to disaster survivors.

Of course there are thresholds. Both too little and too much adversity contribute to negative life outcomes. High levels of distress are associated with poor mental health later in life, yet experiencing next to no adversity also negatively affects overall well-being. To result in positive outcomes, the level of adversity must be somewhere in the middle. The goal isn't to live without challenges, but to be able to move through those that inevitably arise no matter how hard it feels in the moment. Our ability to do so starts with getting comfortable with a few new perspectives, like looking at adversity as sure thing. It is disruption that is constant in life.

YOU'RE NEVER GOING BACK

WE DON'T NEED TO BOUNCE back; we can create anew. In *Master of Change*, author Brad Stulberg highlights our desire for homeostasis (order, disorder, return to order) versus adopting a mindset of allostasis (order, disorder, reorder, as evident in nature) when facing life's highs and hurdles.

Allostasis involves achieving stability through change. Coined by neuroscientist Peter Sterling, allostasis describes the process by which the body anticipates and adapts to varying demands rather than merely responding to them. This approach allows our bodies to adjust our internal parameters to better suit external challenges. Think of the once smooth hands of woodworkers or the feet of long-distance runners (order), where the skin's response to friction and pressure (disorder) is to develop calluses as an adaptive and protective measure (reorder). In the stable career that experiences a major industry shift, the adaptive reordering and growth opportunity is to gain new skills or change careers. These examples illustrate that by embracing change rather than resisting it, we can navigate life's disruptions more effectively, emerging stronger and more adaptable.

Change is good for us. It prompts evolution. Yet our default setting is to resist because it is disruptive to our routines, plans, and goals. It impacts our relationships, health, and sense of self. Change forces us to face uncertainty, and when presented with it, we raise our defenses to remain where we are. What is known is comfortable, no matter how challenging that known may be. It's not easy to muster the significant mental and emotional effort that change requires. The chronic hum of a sinking ship is somehow more tolerable than the acute pain of trying to save ourselves.

If only our tolerance for acute pain were higher. If only we could learn to embrace it, or even gain from it. Some of the greatest adapters to change in mythology and folklore also have a mischievous trickster side to them, such as the coyote in Native American mythology, and Anansi in African folklore. In stories that emphasize adaptability, resourcefulness, and the ever-changing nature of life, Coyote is often portrayed as a shapeshifter. Anansi is a spider known for his cleverness and resilience. His tales emphasize the use of wit and creativity when navigating challenges and change.

We can employ the same skills when facing hurdles by shifting our perspective to one that serves us, like thinking about a challenge as an opportunity to be creative in what the outcome could look like. We can consider gamifying some aspects of the challenge or viewing it with a "challenge accepted" mentality.

Brandon's life was typical for the city he lived in. "I probably would have been working in either the corporate world or the government if it wasn't for everything I went through... The whole thing was go to school, get a job in the government, they can't fire you, you can get out at five every day and do whatever you want. And that's the move, that's the Ottawa dream." He might have stayed on that path, or at least stayed on it longer, if it hadn't been for the major life disruption of being shot.

Like Anansi the spider, Brandon was clever and adaptable. He gamified his progression toward goals during recovery. "Over the first few months of rehab, I put my head down and got to work. The second I was cleared for physio, I was in there five hours a day. Minimum. Every single day of the week. This lasted for about three months, until I slowed down to three to five hours a day, five days a week." Then he started ideating and putting the pieces of a new future together with the creation of his charity, Hit the Ground Running. Brandon shared that "Being in pain allowed me to have a clear mind... I wanted to escape but I was forced to be there, and being forced to be there made me figure out a way forward."

Instead of fearing change and the unknown, plant your perspective flag on the idea of the endless possibilities change provides space for. Change is an opportunity to create a new narrative, new path, new life. It is an invitation to go after something different than what is, and with a little work, you can mold that opportunity to your liking.

MAGIC PILLS, HACKS, AND QUICK FIXES

THE MYTH OF BEING ABLE to take a shortcut to success is a seductive one; social media is full of quick-fix promises. However, the shortest route to success is acknowledging that there isn't one and then putting in the hard, often tedious work. The reality is that most success demands a commitment to consistent, unglamorous actions that compound over time—a lesson that author James Clear brought to us in his ever-popular book, *Atomic Habits*.

Robert Croak, cohost of the *Rich Habits* podcast, often highlights that wealth from investments is about time in the market, not timing the market. "Time in the market" refers to investing an amount monthly over a long period and allowing the funds to compound into wealth. Timing the market is a fool's errand, the lure of a quick wealth fix that leans on a scarcity mindset and rarely, if ever, generates more than a feeling of disappointment. When dissected, hacks and quick fixes reveal themselves as distractions from the authentic work required to make actual progress.

In health, burnout can be an epitome of adversity. Quick fixes seldom address root causes. Instead, resilience-building, self-care, and gradual, sustainable lifestyle changes become the antidote. Is it easy to implement and stay consistent with those changes? No. Would it be easier to take a magic pill? Yes. But that's not the reality we live in. Besides, if we took a magic pill, we'd miss out on the growth, healthy habit development, and pride that comes from putting in the work ourselves.

The burnout I experienced in nursing school took time to heal. It took two years of consistent effort for my cortisol levels to reach a healthy range again and all the other symptoms to fade. At first, the only solution offered was medication for life. My reaction, in a desperate attempt to avoid medication and feel well quickly, was to sink time and money into quick fixes. It's no great surprise that these did not help. Then, between my physician, endocrinologist, and naturopathic doctor, we worked on a plan that was focused on adjusting lifestyle factors. I leaned into the concepts of reordering after disruption and compounding small changes over time. It was an incredibly slow journey to health, but with a little self-compassion, I learned to be grateful for my body and aware that its responses were appropriate reactions to stress. Eventually, medication was no longer recommended because it was no longer needed.

Brandon had a long and challenging road to recovery, one you would expect to be littered with ups and downs, which it was. But according to Brandon, there was a surprising simplicity to his healing process that made it easier for him to stay motivated and reach his goals. Simplicity. A reduction.

The event that landed him in the hospital also freed him to narrow his focus to the singular goal of healing, then running a marathon as proof that he had achieved that goal. "The year I got shot was the best year of my life. It sounds so crazy to say, people don't understand it, but for me it was a walk in the park. It was really hard physically, but it was easy." Meaning that it was structured, with a clear goal, less distraction, and a strong support system. As with the mountaineers and deployed military members I discussed in the last chapter, the ease Brandon described was a result of focusing on a singular goal: He needed to put all his energy into physiotherapy in order to walk again. He had to master basic mobility over hours of grueling and painful exercises, and it was ultimately the compounding small successes of each exercise and mental fortitude that led to him completing a half marathon nine months later, then a full marathon at the thirteen-month mark.

Mountaineers need to stay focused on mountaineering to avoid mishaps, but first they spent hours upon hours learning rope skills, practicing indoors, and rehearsing emergency scenarios. Military members need to stay focused on the mission, but first they spent months if not years mastering basic soldiering skills. There are no magic pills, hacks, or quick fixes for the military, mountaineers, or Brandon. Or for the rest of us.

THINGS DON'T HAPPEN FOR A REASON

When you are going through the worst of times, there's always that one person who tries to console you with "Everything happens for a reason." Although I smile politely when this is offered, my internal urge is to kick them in their well-intentioned shins. The platitude is right up there with "calm down," which, as we all know, is by no means calming. "Things happen for a reason" is something people say when the urge to soothe overcomes the ability to be helpful. I'm sure that I've used this exact statement with others in the past. Things do not happen for a reason; however, we can *add* meaning to what's happened and benefit from that.

There are different ways to add meaning. Depending on the event, we can think of adversity as a catalyst for personal growth and resilience, something that pushes us out of our comfort zones and encourages us to confront and overcome difficulties. This lens facilitates the development of new coping mechanisms and self-awareness. Think of adversity as a somber reminder of how good the good is.

We can view adversity as a springboard that fosters empathy for and understanding of others who are going through their own struggles. Leaning on this perspective assures us that adversity is a natural part of the human condition. It unites us all and reminds us that nobody is immune to life's challenges, regardless of their background, status, or circumstances. Understanding and accepting adversity as a shared human experience can build compassion, support, and a sense of unity within communities and society. We see it in the tight-knit bonds of brotherhood that soldiers weave while deployed, and in the community that gathers to rebuild after a hurricane. These kinds of events present opportunities to reach out, connect, and support one another through the tough times we face, reinforcing the idea that together, we can endure and overcome whatever life throws our way.

Adversity can also be the fuel behind your career, as for many in health care, social services, coaching, fitness, public speaking, and advocacy. I am in this group of meaning-makers. My roles as registered nurse, author, and speaker all have the foundational thread of lived experience with adverse events and other opportunities that the military provided. Those same events are the reason I started writing this book as a collection of life-changing events before massaging it into its current, more helpful state. While I see myself as an accidental speaker on mass casualty preparedness, speaking transmutes challenging lived events and helps me feel like I'm contributing positively to society. Adding meaning to specific events and challenges has helped me use them as powerful ingredients in living well.

After battling with the question of why this happened to him in the first seventy-two hours after the shooting, Brandon answered himself by adding meaning to the event. He decided that it had happened for a reason, that recovery would be hard, and that he would get through it so he could use his story to change lives. After recovery, he started his own charity, Hit the Ground Running, which raises funds to help other shooting survivors heal by paying for physiotherapy and psychotherapy. In his words, "Creating Hit the Ground Running is the closest I could ever come to repaying those who were there for me in my darkest hours. If we are able to bring the same kind of peace and recovery to others going through trauma, I will know that going through all my own personal struggles was worth it."

It is understandable that numbing the pain may be tempting after an event like the one Brandon experienced, but as philosopher Friedrich Nietzsche writes in *On the Genealogy of Morality*, pain is alleviated not through pleasure but meaning-making. Brandon instinctively knew this and requested to withdraw from pain management drugs early[4] so that he could mentally and physically work through the pain himself and draw strength by making meaning of his experience.

While "meaning-making" wasn't a term used by psychiatrist Victor Frankl, he did develop "logotherapy," an approach designed to help others find meaning in life—before his imprisonment in concentration camps during World War II and long before he wrote the classic memoir *Man's Search for Meaning*. In it, Frankl observed that those

---

[4] The request and withdrawment of pain medication was done under the supervision and guidance of his healthcare team. Do not attempt to withdraw from any medication without first consulting medical professionals.

who attached meaning to their future lives had a higher likelihood of surviving the concentration camps.

Meaning-making can be the bridge to whatever direction you would like life to take next, in the way that serves you best. One of the driving concepts in logotherapy is "freedom of will," our ability to choose how we react and our responsibility for those reactions. Our decision to add meaning to adverse events and challenges so that they serve us instead of weighing us down is an act of high agency. As businessman Michael O'Brien stated in a podcast interview with Rich Roll, "Everything is neutral until you label it… you get to decide how you want to look at this."

BEYOND THE LABELS

IN A SOCIETY THAT PATHOLOGIZES regular emotions, eats pop psychology for breakfast like it's actual psychology, and clings heavily to our beloved labels, what if—and try not to cancel me for this one—you're normal, human, and capable? What if you can adapt like nature does? Consider that you are not the single sapling that dies in the fire, but part of the whole forest that constantly adapts to disruptions and rebirths with secondary succession. What if we brought not just one aspect of ourselves to the world, but our full range? A whole forest. A whole human.

Labels have become subtitles in our life's story and often overshadow other aspects of self. On social media, your friend Dave is no longer Dave; he is PTSD Dave, an identity prominently displayed in his username and bio. Lisa lists ADHD and PCOS after her name. Where we used to put academic or professional credentials, we now display diagnoses.

Two thoughts come to mind. First, perhaps we've overcorrected by pathologizing every feeling of discomfort and labeling ordinary human emotions and experiences as disorders. Sadness becomes depression. Nervousness becomes anxiety. Restlessness becomes ADHD. Not every bout of sadness needs a diagnosis. Not every moment of anxiety requires treatment. Sometimes it's just life doing what life does, throwing challenges our way while our minds and bodies react as they are designed to. It's easy to get caught up in "fixing" ourselves. Even when life is going well, we are inundated with messages about improvement. Frameworks that promise machine-like productivity. Health trackers to optimize our bodies' functionality. Coaches for work, life, relationships, and everything else under the sun. Social media advertisements and cold calls over direct messaging with cure-alls for woes we didn't even realize we had. The self-help sections at bookstores have exploded; Marketdata reports that over forty million books were sold under this category in 2022, with the subcategory of personal transformation, relationships, and motivation being top sellers. They also report that personal coaching is up a whopping 77 percent from 2020 to 2022, making it a $2 billion-plus industry, and the Noom weight loss app generates over $400 million a year.

The second thought is that there are absolutely diagnoses that require treatment. Of course there are. And often, labels can bring a sense of community and understanding to the table and open doors to programs and support. This is an invitation to explore self-attached labels. Is adopting that label and etching it so firmly to your identity serving you? Is it keeping you safe or stuck? Ultimately, whether a label helps or hinders you is yours to evaluate.

Calibrating your baseline is an opportunity to create your own reality by acknowledging that adversity is normal, the long game is the quick hack, you can choose the meaning you attach to your experiences, and there are consequences to the labels we give ourselves.

Every disruption in life becomes an opportunity to lead yourself forward. But in order to do so—beyond having the perspectives and attitudes that serve you—it helps to be standing on solid ground when these adverse events occur. The next step is to master the mundane.

CHAPTER 4

Master the Mundane

Good and evil both increase at compound interest. That is why little decisions you and I make every day are of such infinite importance.
—C.S. Lewis

IMAGINE IF SOMEONE HAD THE audacity to tell you how to tie your shoelaces. You'd think it was a joke. And what if you were an athlete being told how to put on socks? Laughable. Get out of here. Except that's exactly how legendary UCLA Bruins basketball coach John Wooden began each season. It seems ridiculous, but Wooden believed that excellence stems from mastering the fundamentals, like putting on socks and tying your shoes to avoid blisters. His success spoke volumes about his methods: UCLA won ten NCAA championships in twelve years.

Japanese swordsman and strategist Miyamoto Musashi highlighted the importance of mastering the basics. In his *The Book of Five Rings*, he promoted the rigorous practice of fundamental techniques, stating that true mastery comes from perfecting basic skills until they become second nature. He reportedly had an undefeated record of winning more than sixty duels.

Wooden and Musashi aren't the only ones hyper-focusing on the fundamentals to achieve success. One of the most successful investors in history, Warren Buffett, built his fortune by focusing on basic investing principles taught by his mentor, Benjamin Graham, and resisting the temptation to chase trends. In 2025, his net worth was over $147 billion.

A professional athlete coach, legendary samurai, and expert investor all found their greatest success in mastering the mundane. The approach is so simple that it seems absurd, yet it is a proven, powerful winning strategy. It is our winning strategy as well, because unless you've mastered the basics, you're still not running the show. And if you're not running the show, adversity will. It'll see that gap in your foundation and trip you up like a champ.

WHAT WILL BE WILL BE—OR WILL IT?

WE WANT TO GET AWAY with skipping sleep, spending hours glued to a screen, and eating what is convenient. We *need* to. We have businesses to build, kids to raise, bills to pay. There is no stopping this train.

It really doesn't matter if you skip a weight training once or twice. I mean, if you miss today, then tomorrow, might as well scratch the week and start again Monday. Or maybe you never miss a workout. Maybe you're a beast of a human, admired for your tenacity, but can't seem to get the results you want lately. The obvious response is to double down. Work out harder. Keep going. You can take it. It doesn't matter that you are on screens all day and answering work emails in bed late at night because you can rest later; this is just a surge, albeit a never-ending one. It doesn't matter that you don't have a core group of friends to unwind with, or perhaps you do but haven't seen them in ages because other people are too busy for that too.

Except all of this matters.

Deep down, we know it does. Yet we all sacrifice the fundamentals, the foundation of our well-being, until one day we find ourselves with nothing left because this level of self-inflicted harm is unsustainable. Look at us, stealing from our future selves and thinking we'll get away with it. That's cute.

No one gets away with it. Without a strong foundation to lean on when adversity comes next, as it always does, we're on unsteady ground. We can lean on reduction to right the path, but to make our journey sustainable, we have to follow up with learning to tie our shoes, no matter how elementary that seems. This helps us create our own "luck."

One of my favorite professional explorers to follow online, Mike Horn, is a South African-born Swiss who takes on adventures that most of us only dream about. He said this about luck: *"Pourquoi je crois dans la chance, tout simplement parce que il faut aussi ca pour que je puisse faire ce que je fais. Mais la chance il faux aussi un peu la provoque."* This translates roughly to: "Why do I believe in luck, simply put, I have to in order to do what I do. But luck, you have to nudge her a little." A beautiful sentiment illustrating agency, our participation in life, and outcomes. We can nudge luck toward our favor by mastering the mundane. And we will master the mundane because it is a better way forward for us, our loved ones, and our community. Let's start by clearing a few obstacles.

UNALIGNED FEELINGS AND ACTIONS

Ever listen to interviews with high achievers who get up at 5:00 a.m. and go for a run before starting their day? They do it regardless of their desire to stay in bed. This seems to most of us like an unrelatable superpower. A mutant gene. There is some truth to that; a 2019 meta-analysis of data from 30,000 twins suggests that approximately 60 percent of our willpower, the ability to control ourselves, is genetic.

But what if you weren't stuck with low self-control because of a strong genetic predisposition? What if you had decent self-control in some areas but not others? What if you could exercise your brain to become the type of person who consistently does the actions that are good for you even if you don't feel like it?

Self-control is not just genes, though, and you're not stuck. In a social media post, entrepreneur Leila Hormozi sums up the feeling nicely: "You want to change your life, and it just feels really hard. I want you to remember that the reason you are not changing is because the cost of remaining the same is not yet higher than the cost of change."

The cost analysis Hormozi is referencing is done in the anterior mid-cingulate cortex (aMCC), a hub in the brain that interfaces with several networks. What we really want to appreciate is its role in managing effort, resolving conflict, and motivating behavior. The aMCC is activated when you push yourself to do something you don't like doing or find challenging. It weighs the potential rewards and discomfort associated with the action you need to take to achieve a certain goal. Researchers use words like *willpower, tenacity, perseverance,* and *resolve* when discussing the aMCC, the exact qualities we need to cultivate in order to master the mundane. Lucky us: The aMCC is something we can exercise, grow, and strengthen.

We can activate and exercise the aMCC by simply doing the things we find challenging and that are outside of our normal routine, like getting up early to go for a run, or learning a new language. Even doing taxes, if that's something you loathe and find difficult as much as I do. This activation involves processing and regulating cognitive and emotional aspects of goal-directed behavior. Regularly engaging in these types of activities can promote growth of the aMCC leading an increased capacity to handle difficult tasks and improved resilience, persistence, and willpower. So next time your feelings are about to impede your action, try doing it anyway and start developing your ability to endure short-term discomfort for long-term benefits.

THE LURE OF OPTIMIZATION

Ask any software developer in the world if they've heard the quote "Premature optimization is the root of all evil" from Donald Knuth,[5] and they will likely say yes. On the surface, the quote is a warning. The full quote, however, is, "We should forget about small efficiencies, say about 97 percent of the time: premature optimization is the root of all evil. Yet we should not pass up our opportunities in that critical 3 percent." It is not a warning against optimization, but against pursuing it too soon and in big leaps.

A similar warning is found in "You can't out-train a bad diet," a common refrain amongst fitness professionals. It reminds us to focus on nutrition as a foundational element to improving fitness. Physical training will help you gain strength and mobility, but if your diet isn't up to par, that growth will be stunted. Not to mention the compounding internal effects of poor nutrition.

Yet we are mesmerized by the lure of optimization in big leaps in computer science, health, and other areas—like the entrepreneur who spends $17,000 on a slick new website

---

[5] There is some debate about whether Donald Knuth first said this, or Sir Tony Hoare, or if Hoare said this and was quoting Knuth.

out of envy of the competition without having the sales to support such a steep upgrade or even fully evaluating its necessity (true story, I did this), the cost being wasted financial and temporal resources and a lot of frustration. The incremental step could have been polling clients to determine which elements would add to their experience, then adding one of the requested elements and monitoring sales trends. Another incremental step could have been implementing the Profit First strategy created by entrepreneur and author Mike Michalowicz, an effective financial approach that, among other things, stops you from overspending in your business. I did this last one after the website faux pas, and it saved my business.

It also looks like the nonathlete who buys a $3,000 road bike before even trying a triathlon to see if they like the sport. Again, I did this, and it not only cost a dent in the wallet but my pride after not finishing the race (or any other since).

It's all of us implementing complex training, business, and life plans before we've taken care of the simple things. Premature optimization can sabotage our efforts to advance by wasting our time, energy, and resources. It can also lead to a good amount of discouragement.

When is it good to optimize? When your foundation is solid and it's taken you as far as it can take you. When you reach that point, ask yourself a few clarifying questions:

- Is there a genuine need to optimize?

- What will I miss out on by going with a smaller step?
- What is the cost of implementing this optimization?
- What is this optimization's return on investment (ROI)?
- Can this be tested on a smaller scale before I implement it fully?

Master of Change author Brad Stulberg shared in an article that "peak performance is not about supplements, cold plunges, or fancy protocols. It's about a steadfast commitment to nailing the fundamentals of your craft for years and having the right people around you. With consistency and community, you can become very good at nearly anything."

Remember that the quickest way to optimize your health is to master the basics. The quickest way to optimize your finances is to master the basics. The quickest way to optimize your professional skills is to master the basics. Otherwise, you risk being the Titanic, decked out with lavish details but missing the fundamental requirements of lifeboats and safety measures so you can deal with an emergency when it arises.

INABILITY TO NOTICE RESULTS

CONSISTENCY IS KEY. OKAY, BUT if I do twenty-five push-ups a day, I expect to see defined biceps as soon as my arms reach full extension on the twenty-fifth rep on the first day. No? That's not how things work? Logically we know it isn't, yet is there anything more frustrating or disheartening than working on a goal for an extended period and *not* seeing results?

On the *Finding Mastery* podcast with Dr. Gervais, Robert Greene, author of *The 48 Laws of Power*, spoke about his recovery from stroke in 2018: " I had this idea that okay, in a year I'll be swimming again, I'll be walking again, but it didn't work out that way… Normally when you go to the gym and you try something new, you lift weights, you see results in a couple of weeks and it keeps you excited… This, you see results in eight months, a year, if at all. You hardly ever see results. Other people might notice a slight change, but you don't feel it in your body. How do you keep going? I do [physical] therapy every single day… How do you keep going when you don't see results, right?"

It can be hard to visualize long-term outcomes and benefits. Doing the math helps bring the big picture and potential into focus.

Instant gratification would be winning the lotto, but you can invest five hundred dollars per month starting at age eighteen and have $1.4 million when you reach sixty-five. That's a total of $282,000 in contributions for over $1.4 million. This is assuming a conservative average interest rate of six percent each year. If you check the interest growth at the beginning it may feel like you're getting nowhere, but the power of consistent effort and compound interest pays off in the end. Finance is the simplest example I can use to illustrate my point, but it doesn't stop there.

Walking 12,500 steps a day equals walking approximately 2,157 miles (3,468 kilometers) a year. That's about eighty-two marathons and just shy of the distance between New York City and Los Angeles. Walking increases cardiac health and bone strength and promotes healthy weight, leading to decreased risk of chronic diseases such as heart disease, osteoporosis, and type 2 diabetes.

Meditating for ten minutes a day adds up to about sixty hours of meditation a year, which will certainly improve mental clarity and reduce stress.

Regularly attending networking events and engaging with community groups can lead to meaningful, long-term relationships that benefit your personal and professional life. If you attend one event per month over five years, you can potentially connect with sixty new people.

Reading can reduce stress, introduce new perspectives, and broaden your knowledge base. Enjoy consuming ten pages of a book daily and you'll end up reading about 3,650 pages a year. If each book averages three hundred pages, that's a solid twelve books a year.

Compounding works with the negative as well. The average North American scrolls social media for just over two hours a day. That's more than thirty days of scrolling per year. The average lifespan in the US is seventy-six. Imagine: If you got your first phone at eighteen and had an average lifespan, you'd spend nearly five years of your life staring at your phone.

Consuming an extra (above your specific nutritional requirements) two hundred calories a day, just ten calories more than one sixteen-ounce vanilla blonde latte at Starbucks, equals 73,000 extra calories annually and a possible twenty-pound weight gain (if no other factors like exercise are involved). While we're taking about that latte, six dollars a day amounts to $2,190 over the course of a year.

Negative compounding is just as much of a motivator in mastering the mundane as positive compounding. I never noticed the impact of small actions until I stopped doing them. In fact, it took a full decade for me to see that my small, seemingly inconsequential actions—like staying connected to a group of friends with shared core experiences, exercising daily, and taking pride in how I dressed before going out—actually had a profound positive effect on my life. At the time, I thought I was lacking in these areas and failing to advance in any noticeable way. My friendships weren't close-knit enough, my fitness level high enough, or my clothes stylish enough. And then these rituals fell by the wayside when I went to university and, admittedly, for years after I finished the program. Omitting those daily practices created a decline in my fitness, friendships, and level of self-care that had a ripple effect on other areas of my life. As author Robert Greene says in the *Finding Mastery* podcast, "You just have to be patient because, as my wife explained to me, if I didn't do that hour and a half of therapy, I would have degraded. I would have lost. I wouldn't have kept at least a level of stasis."

Now I understand that the value of small, consistent actions is not always in progressive results you can't see, but also in negative effects they help you to avoid.

If you're struggling with not seeing immediate results from your efforts, try considering the consequences of not taking the action, visualizing or calculating the long-term results and benefits, or using a tracker so you can see how far you've come. Remember, you are leading by example. The ripple effect of taking care of yourself can impact your children, friends, coworkers, etc. Now that you're aware of the obstacles you can clear, it's time for those big lever-pulls.

BIG LEVER-PULLS

"Your cholesterol is high. Let's look at statins," the resident physician said while reviewing my latest lab results. Before I had a chance to say anything, my GP walked in.

"No, she does lifestyle changes first," he said. "Medication if we need to, but only after she tries changing a few things."

He always lets me work on myself first, allowing the responsibility for changes to fall on my shoulders, which only increases my deep sense of agency.

When I got home from that appointment, I read about a two-year study that found that high-intensity exercise in sedentary mid-lifers improved their heart health by 18 percent.

I laced up my sneakers the next day.

Lifestyle medicine organizations in Canada, the UK, and the US agree on six pillars of a healthy lifestyle: nutrition, physical activity, stress management, restorative sleep, social connection, and avoidance of risky substance use. These six pillars are the biggest levers to pull in support of your well-being and ability to handle adversity. My friend Joyce, a senior medical doctor in the UK, once told me that if people "started to master the fundamentals, I would have no patients left to treat." What a great aim for us all: a better, healthier life that lowers overall healthcare needs.

Chances are you already know how to sleep, eat, move, connect, chill, and how risky substance use can be, but do you realize how big a lever-pull mastering these fundamentals is?

I am fascinated by all things adventure, adversity, and well-being, and yet the considerable impact of getting the basics down pat still surprises me. As Dr. Uma Naidoo, a psychiatrist and professional chef, articulated on the *Rich Roll* podcast: "Lifestyle and nutrition are the one remediable factor across all chronic diseases. We know this." Remediable factor. Something we can do something about it. And we will, by focusing on these big lever-pulls.

The American Academy of Sleep Medicine, like most health organizations, recommends that adults get over seven hours (usually between seven and nine hours) of sleep per night. A 2022 report from the CDC shows that in America, depending on the state, 30–46 percent of adults are not getting enough sleep. In Canada, over 17 percent of adults suffer the same fate.

Sleep is a vital aspect of our physical, mental, and emotional health. Did you know that getting less than seven hours can contribute to depression, metabolic disease, and cardiac disease? It contributes to missed work hours, too. In 2020, that represented an annual economic loss of $500 million for Canada. Insufficient sleep, even if you get between four and six hours, increases your odds of being responsible for a vehicle accident by 1.3–2.9 times the average of a well-slept person. Operating on less than four hours? Your odds are *fifteen times* higher than average.

"I'll rest later" isn't as easy or sufficient as you think, either. According to a 2016 study, it takes four days of consistent, quality sleep to make up for only one hour of sleep debt.

I've never had an issue with sleeping enough; I sack out for seven and a half to nine hours a night. I am terribly inconsistent with my bedtime, though. What works for me is setting an evening alarm as a reminder to start getting ready for sleep, a tip I picked up from Dr. Trevor Kashey, an incredible human with a biochemistry PhD who runs cognitive nutrition programs. The alarm is my cue to switch gears and start preparing for bed instead of getting sucked into watching another episode of whatever television series I'm currently indulging in at the cost of consistent, quality sleep.

There are two lessons I've learned when it comes to mastering the mundane:

1. The simpler the better, and
2. You have to keep trying.

What do I mean by that? Let's look at the remaining lifestyle pillars: nutrition, physical activity, stress management, social connection, and avoiding risky substance use.

Simplifying nutrition might look like eating the same foods all week, or only focusing on portions, or paying for a meal service—whatever is easiest for you and reduces your cognitive stress load and barriers to compliance. With physical activity, it might be switching to a more manual job, doing body weight exercises, or rucking (carrying additional weight in a backpack) while you walk the dog.

Social connections can be through work, sports, or joining an interest group. Or, if you don't find a place to build social connections right away, create it. When I left the military, I felt, well, a little lost. Like I didn't fit in anywhere. One of the first things I did was start a local hiking resource business, girlgonegood.com, and let like-minded folks with shared values find me. Eventually, it became a strong, engaged community.

Being a part of a community and socializing matters. A 2023 study by Wang, Gao, Han, et al. found that social isolation increases the risk of early death from any cause by a whopping 32 percent. The reality of this statistic is so hard-hitting that community events, friends, and social opportunities were factors in my last move and will be in any future ones.

In today's polarizing and often isolating world, we underrate the power of engaging with people outside our circle, yet we thrive in community. It provides aspects of well-being like relatedness, affiliation, and social contact. It opens the doors to other experiences and points of view, broadening our own perceptions. Talking to strangers gives us practice with social engagement. The bonus is that we can discover strengths within our communities to leverage during times of need and provide the same in return. It's good to know that Nancy three doors down is a doctor, Frank the barista is also a master gardener, and dog-walking Doug can fix just about anything mechanical. Better yet, we can teach and gain insights from each other.

HARD, NOT COMPLICATED

REDUCTION IS A TOOL. CALIBRATING baseline is a shift in perspective. Mastering the mundane is the minimum requirement to fall back on during hard times and the foundation from which a big life is launched. Nutrition, physical activity, stress management, restorative sleep, social connection, and avoidance of risky substance use: The fundamentals are neither glamorous nor complicated, but with enough effort, they become the stabilizers that keep us on even ground when life gets shaky.

CHAPTER 5

Activate High Agency

Man is nothing else but what he makes of himself.
—Jean-Paul Sartre

How is it that taking drastic measures, like jumping on a plane and flying halfway around the world to seek out a healer, can seem like a better decision than sitting at home in discomfort and looking inward? The latter would have been cheaper. Safer. Logical. Instead, I traveled to Bali by myself to visit Mr. Ketut, then famous as the healer in Elizabeth Gilbert's book *Eat, Pray, Love*. If I could get a glimpse of the future, maybe I could figure out who I needed to be now.

Waiting with me to see Mr. Ketut were three Americans—a couple happily playing cards with their two-year-old daughter—and three Australians. The Americans went first, then the Australians, and after three hours of waiting, it was my turn.

Mr. Ketut started by stating that I was "very, very pretty," that he was "very, very happy to meet" me, and that my lifeline was "very, very good." I'd live to be a hundred. My heart line was also apparently very good.

"Do you have boyfriend?" he asked. When I answered no, he stood in mock shock and disbelief. "Yes you do," he replied. I didn't see the need to argue. "You will be married, long married, until the end of your lives. It'll be a happy marriage; you are a smart woman."

He read my knees, telling me how healthy I was, then turned me around to read my back and told me I had the energy of the lotus flower. All similar, if not exactly the same as what he told the Americans and Australians before me.

I left no further ahead than when I went in. It was the equivalent of buying a lotto ticket instead of investing for retirement or hoping the latest fad diet would work instead of adapting to a healthier lifestyle. This was a disrupted-sense-of-self quick-fix attempt and, admittedly, not my last. Over the years, I've been to all sorts of healers, psychics, and readers, trying to decipher the future and my place in it. As much as I enjoy indulging in faith, folklore, and fairytales, most of their advice was that life is a bumpy road we are all more than capable of traveling if only we take more time to look inward.

We don't need to know the future. We need to know ourselves.

UNLOCK AWARENESS

The bedrock of being a High Agency Human—someone with intentionality, the desire to achieve, and the ability to act effectively—is self-awareness. There are two broadly defined categories of self-awareness, internal and external. Think of internal self-awareness as the clarity with which we see ourselves and external self-awareness as how well we understand how others see us. Without self-awareness, we can't accurately gauge our internal landscape, understand our motivations, or recognize how our actions affect us and the world around us.

Both ancient philosophers, like the Stoics we love to quote, and modern researchers highlight the link between self-awareness and human agency. The Stoic philosophers of ancient Greece, like Socrates, Plato, and Aristotle, emphasized self-awareness as a prerequisite for mastering one's life.

In *Courage is Calling*, author Ryan Holiday observes that "There is no one who has achieved greatness without wrestling with their own doubts, anxieties, limitations, and demons." High agency takes the same route as courage. It includes becoming aware of, confronting, and mastering the internal self, including doubts, anxieties, and limiting beliefs that might otherwise hold us back. For the Stoics, personal responsibility and control over one's inner state were the cornerstones of a virtuous and fulfilling life. We often hear the motivational refrains "You can do hard things" and "We cannot control external events, only our response to them," but this level of resilience and grit requires a clear, deep level of self-awareness.

Modern psychological research echoes the Stoics' understanding of the importance of self-awareness. Studies on emotional intelligence and self-regulation show that folks who possess a high degree of self-awareness are better able to manage their emotions, leading to improved decision-making, resilience, and personal effectiveness, the hallmarks of high agency. Psychologist Daniel Goleman, a pioneer in emotional intelligence, shares that self-awareness is the foundation upon which other critical life skills are built, including self-regulation, empathy, and social skills. He states that self-awareness "means having a deep understanding of one's emotions, strengths, weaknesses, needs, and drives."

In the real world, hindered agency compounded by lack of awareness could present in various ways, including a decline in health, financial instability, or a lack of progression toward goals. Let's imagine Mark, who is constantly stressed at his highly demanding job. He starts experiencing physical symptoms like stubborn weight gain, insomnia, and stomach issues but attributes these to age or genetics and decides that he simply needs to push harder. Mark is unaware of how stress is impacting his body and overall well-being. He doesn't realize that his body is reacting to chronic stress because he's never taken the time to notice how his emotional state correlates with his physical health. Without this awareness, Mark may not adopt stress-relief practices, seek professional help, or set boundaries at work, leading to a further decline in his health. This lack of self-awareness prevents him from taking control of his health and making the changes necessary to improve his well-being.

Another scenario involves Maria, who is constantly stressed about money. No matter how much she earns, she always finds herself living paycheck to paycheck and racking up credit card debt. Maria lacks awareness of her spending habits and emotional triggers. She uses retail therapy to cope with stress and boredom but isn't conscious of this pattern. Maria knows she treats herself when stressed but doesn't track the spending or realize how much it is keeping her in debt. Without this awareness, she is unable to break the cycle and make more intentional financial decisions, leaving her stuck in a pattern of financial instability. Maria's situation is common; I was Maria and continue to fight not to be her.

The last fictional scenario involves Shawn, who always feels like he's spinning his wheels. He starts new hobbies, sets goals, and begins new projects, but rarely sees anything through to completion. He often feels lost and unsure and is unaware that he sets goals based on external inputs instead of checking internally to discover what's right for him. One scroll through social media is all it takes to see what he "should" be doing. Without awareness of what drives him,

Shawn keeps switching gears, never gaining momentum or clarity in any one direction. This lack of alignment between his actions and values undermines his sense of agency, leaving him feeling directionless and disempowered.

Lacking insight into why we behave a certain way, what drives us, or how we react under pressure limits our ability to act with purpose, make intentional decisions, or adapt to changing circumstances.

MASTER LANGUAGE

WHEN IT COMES TO ADVERSITY, we use words like *trauma, hurdle, challenge, overwhelm, catastrophe, distress, hardship, burnout,* and *stress*. They all mean very different things; are we using them correctly? When we use these words, are we describing true adversity or things we don't like, don't want to do, or inconvenience us? Is it adversity or normal life? Why is it high life or bust? Are we saying "overwhelmed" when we mean "stressed"? What is the definition of each?

It's not that what we go through isn't significant, it's that we misuse words without even realizing we are doing it. If we can bring awareness to the language we use, we can strengthen the stories we tell ourselves for our own benefit. Take the word "overwhelmed" as an example. American scientist, writer, and meditation teacher Jon Kabat-Zinn stated in a 2019 article that the word "overwhelm" describes a state where "Our lives are unfolding faster than the human nervous system or psyche can handle." Kabat-Zinn goes on to propose that the only solution to overwhelm is to reset with nothingness. Actual nothingness. Can you imagine? Sounds a little, well, extreme. Overwhelm must be a hell of a state to require nothingness as a treatment.

I've used and misused the word often; I know I have. I've used it to incorrectly describe being overscheduled, stressed, and tired. Now I try to catch myself, since announcing overwhelm means I'm beyond my ability to manage the current load. Completely beyond. It means I am unable to meet any further demands or requests; my body has unapologetically forced me to stop. Even while I was working through burnout, being in a state of absolute overwhelm was rare.

If I say I'm experiencing a stress, hardship, hurdle, or challenge, then I'm expressing that I'm having a hard time but it can be overcome. Crisis and distress communicate that an immediate threat exists and attention is required to resolve it.

Using language reflective of our experience in the stories we tell ourselves and others has greater consequence for our well-being than one might assume. Why does using the right language matter? One strong reason is that our internal and external dialogue create psychological effects that impact our outcomes. In a 2019 study of the effects of verbal encouragement on performance outcomes in relation to ankle stability, participants who were given positive verbal encouragement experienced a perceived increase in motivation that directly impacted their outcomes. Another 2019 study, on the impact of word choice on perceived pain, supports motivational priming theory: The use of negative or neutral words prior to a physical procedure increased the brain's perception of pain and the patient's overall pain rating.

If the words we use have such significant power, imagine the impact we can have when we weave them together and direct them toward others.

"The American people have faced other grave crises in their history—with American courage, and with American resolution. They will do no less today." These were the calm, steady words spoken by President Franklin D. Roosevelt on September 11, 1941 during one of his "fireside chats" that aired over the radio. Reading through the transcripts, it is easy to appreciate how Roosevelt mastered language to ease public anxiety and promote a deep and unified resolve during the Great Depression and World War II. He delivered each carefully written fireside chat in an unscripted, engaging style. The resonance was clear, and listeners wrote in with praise. Each broadcast elicited hundreds of thousands of letters and telegrams from the public.

When we take ownership of narratives, we take ownership of our identity and impact—a rebellious act of agency in itself.

ASSUME OWNERSHIP

IN THE THICK OF EVERY hurdle, whether a basement flood, job loss, or challenging relationship, after the initial gut punch and a few expletives, there is no escaping the thought that *I'm the one who got myself here*: a simple yet powerful acknowledgment that allows us to expand into an ownership mindset, goes beyond narrative and identity, and includes responsibility over outcomes. In *Extreme Ownership*, retired Navy SEAL and author Jocko Willink writes: "The leader must own everything in his or her world. There is no one else to blame. The leader must acknowledge mistakes and admit failures, take ownership of them, and develop a plan to win."

When Brandon (the shooting survivor turned charity CEO) described his childhood, he mentioned that his father and grandfather, both big influences in his life, were highly principled guys. "They hold the people around them to high standards, and it's because there is this belief in everyone around them. From the time I was five years old, I was told that the world is mine. It wasn't a family where, like, 'My kid is the sun, the moon, and the stars.' It was more like, 'You got all the tools and it's on you.'"

"That kind of understanding and ownership must have given you a sense of agency," I interjected.

"Yeah," Brandon continued, "I think that was a great attitude to learn as a kid because I learned that I was capable of anything. But also, because I was capable of anything,

I was totally capable of screwing it all up. It was on me either way."

There is an immense freedom in taking ownership. It reinforces your sense that you impact what comes next through your decisions and actions.

One of the tenets of military leadership, from the most junior officer to the highest general, is to lead by example in a manner that doesn't just reflect well in team environments, but also demonstrates integrity when no one is watching. An ownership mindset includes taking responsibility and acting with integrity. If you were recorded twenty-four hours a day, would you be proud of the playback? Could you own your actions?

BREAK CAGES

IMAGINE A GROUP OF PRISONERS who have been chained underground and are stuck looking at the cave wall in front of them their entire lives. Behind the prisoners is a low wall, and behind that wall is a fire. Between the fire and the low wall are both stationary and moving objects that create shadows on the large cave wall, the only wall the prisoners can see. The prisoners believe that the shadows are real and that they are the only possible real things, there is no world beyond. If you're not familiar with it, this is how Socrates' "Allegory of the Cave," recorded by Plato in *The Republic*, begins. It is a strange account with many questions to ponder. What if one of the prisoners were freed? What would he do? What would he believe? Would he adjust to the outside world? Thrive, even? Or, as Socrates concluded, would the prisoner return to the safety and comfort of the known, the cave?

We might like to imagine that the prisoner would liberate the rest and they would all walk out into the awe-inspiring final scenes of *The Sound of Music*, free and ready to lead fulfilling lives. Wouldn't that be preferable to going back to the dark, restricting, uninspiring cave—ideal, even? It's easy to have the answers when we're on the outside looking in. But what if we are in a cave and don't realize it? In a world with unlimited access to information, perhaps it's not a cave at all, but a cage with invisible bars that we put in place ourselves.

Our cage bars are not constructed of iron or steel, but of beliefs, cognitive biases, and psychological conditioning. Once recognized, our malleable internal barriers can be removed.

The imagery of cages is common in metaphors for the psychological restraints we face, whether self-imposed or imposed by others or systems. You can find terms like "mental cage" and "internal cage" scattered throughout different articles, papers, and online posts. This vivid imagery illustrates psychological concepts that might otherwise be indigestible. What do these cages look like in our daily lives? They often take forms so familiar that we rarely question them. Let's explore a few of the more common ones.

1.

The Cage of Comparison: Measuring yourself against someone else's life metrics. For example, this could look like comparing fitness gains someone else posted on social media to your own progress or lack thereof and allowing that comparison to weigh you down (if it pushes you forward, it is not a cage). Another example is watching friends build businesses faster or take trips that you can only dream about. This cage is the scroll through social media while thinking *What am I doing wrong?* The hidden cost is that, instead of staying focused on your own progress and wins, you can waste time, energy, and motivation chasing someone else's blueprint.

2.

The Cage of Compliance: Defaulting to others' expectations, not what's aligned. You have achieved everything expected of you, what you were told to achieve: the higher educational degree, respectable career path, and socially accepted life. Everything that should equal fulfillment yet doesn't. The high agency reframe is to consider what you actually want life to look like—and to remember that you don't need permission to pivot.

3.

The Cage of Control: Believing if you don't do it all, it won't get done. You're the one whose absence would mean work falls apart, the one who does it all and more. The person people call when they need help or want to know how to get things done. Delegation feels risky and rest, well, that's impossible. On the surface, this may look like high agency, but it has the hidden cost of creating resentment and negative health effects. The high agency move is to intentionally let go so you can move forward, stronger.

The list of cages could go on. If life feels scripted, or if you've ever felt like you can't speak up, start over, or slow down—even when no one's stopping you—you may be trapped in a cage. And it can be dismantled. The method is simple: Identify it, challenge it, and exit it.

Identify it by naming it: *This is a cage.* Challenge it by intentionally disrupting the current internal narrative with questions like, *Is this a truth or a rule? Did I choose this or inherit it? Is this helping or hindering my goals? If I didn't care what others thought, would I still be doing this?* And exit by making sure that the next step you take aligns with your personal goals, building upon your highly agentic identity through action.

BEYOND THE OBVIOUS

TWO BICYCLE MECHANICS FROM DAYTON, Ohio with no formal engineering degrees, no government grants, and no big names behind them made the impossible possible. What they had was innate curiosity and the kind of high agency thinking that refuses to quit. While better-funded scientists clung to theories and failed in labs, Wilbur and Orville Wright relentlessly tested their concepts for flight in the real world. They failed, adjusted, flew further, adjusted again, and failed again. In 1903, they became the first humans to achieve powered, controlled flight—not because they were born geniuses, but because they thought differently and acted persistently.

They didn't wait for perfect conditions or seek permission. They got clear on the outcome and worked backward from there. That's what high agency looks like in motion.

We tend to think that the path to agency is paved with hard work, good habits, and a strong mindset. There is truth in that. But the real breakthroughs, the exponential gains in life, come from venturing beyond the obvious. High Agency Humans aren't just gritty. They're curious. Strategic. Unconventional. They question systems, test assumptions, and refuse to play by rules that don't serve them.

Beyond mastering language, assuming ownership, and breaking cages, here are additional ways to increase agency in your own life.

Practice cognitive flexibility and orthogonal thinking. High agency thinkers can shift perspectives, reinterpret events, and update their beliefs without losing their sense of self. This is called cognitive flexibility, and research shows that it's key to problem-solving, resilience, and emotional regulation. A complimentary cognitive approach is orthogonal thinking, the ability to connect seemingly unconnected independent variables to achieve new insight.

It's looking at things differently, from another angle. Train your mind by playing devil's advocate with your own opinions and beliefs, regularly asking yourself if the opposite could be true, and seeking out people and content with opposing thoughts.

Practice cognitive reappraisal and allow space to process as a strategy for emotional regulation. There are multiple possible reactions to stressful, negative situations. Cognitive reappraisal is a way of adjusting your emotional response by carefully changing your thoughts around the event to produce a more positive, helpful outcome. Train your response by taking a moment to consider any positive outcomes, whether there are lessons to be learned, and if there is anything from this experience you can use toward future goals.

Surround yourself with High Agency Humans. If we are the sum of the people we hang around with most, let the bulk of our people be High Agency Humans—with some of them operating at higher levels than us in varied areas of life so that we can learn from, encourage, and push each other into higher levels of living. High agency people are easy to identify: Look for the ones you would call in an emergency, the ones who take on new challenges without fear or despite their fear, and the ones who always land on their feet.

After reaching a dead end with the healer in Bali, I packed my bags and headed to Borneo to hike Malaysia's tallest peak, Mount Kinabalu. Surely the mountain would test my fortitude and reveal answers. It tested my fortitude alright, every single steep-as-all-get-out step, but I didn't feel any wiser. Then I traveled to a remote island in Thailand and spent time journaling in solitude. Surely journaling would reveal the "ahas" I needed. The opportunity to word-vomit on each page was a relief, but insightful? I still wasn't seeing it.

I didn't find the solution on this trip, but I did make the first step. My adventures supported what I had already concluded with the healer: I needed to explore, question, and expand myself if I wanted to move forward.

High agency isn't a steady state; it's a practice, a commitment to act with intention. Even when the ground shakes, move forward—not because it is easy, but because it is yours to do.

CHAPTER 6

Boost Protective Buffers

Invest in preparedness, not in prediction.
—Nassim Taleb

Looking down at his muddy boots, then up and around him, Ron realized that he was, in fact, lost. Not lost like when there's a pop quiz on a subject you barely know or you can't find where you left your bike after school; no, this scrappy fifteen-year-old dressed in fatigues, a white tank top, and bush hat was lost among giants in the thick of British Columbia's Golden Ears Park. The second-growth forest of mature western hemlock, western red cedar and Douglas fir towered over him, their canopies obscuring sections of sky. Leaves rustled in the wind. He could hear a trickle of water off in the distance. Any other kid would have felt panic rising within them, but Ron felt calm. A bit pleased, even.

Ron had been preparing for moments like this since about five years earlier, when he began filling empty two-liter pop bottles with water and pinching random food items from his mother's kitchen to squirrel away in the basement just in case. This was not without reason. He lives in Southwestern BC, which experiences approximately four hundred earthquakes per year according to Natural Resources Canada. It is the most seismically active region in Canada. So, when young Ron heard media warnings about "the big one" possibly hitting Vancouver and that citizens should prepare, he did just that. He didn't quite understand expiration dates, but he knew enough not to pick perishable food. A can of corn would go missing one day, perhaps a bag of chips the next. In his mind, the reallocation was for the greater good, though more than once the missing supplies disrupted his mother's meal plans.

After joining the cadets at the age of thirteen, Ron was introduced to the military kit they brought on camping trips and thought, *Hey, I don't have anything like that.* The secret basement emergency stash quickly expanded to include waterproof matches, tarps, and warm layers. When the other kids at cadet camp didn't eat all their MREs (meals-ready-to-eat, with a five-year shelf life), Ron collected them to add to his personal preparedness collection of kit and food goods.

Whenever there was a power outage at home, Ron would run down to get the candles, matches, and flashlight with a sense of "Don't worry, Mom, I got this"—and he did, to the degree that any kid could. Knowing he had and could use these items created proof of his capability and built his confidence.

Getting lost was never part of the plan. And this was supposed to be an easy, straightforward hike. Yet here he was, completely and unexpectedly disoriented in the woods. Shrugging his shoulders to hike up his plain black backpack while tightening the straps, Ron started bushwhacking through vegetation and climbing over fallen trees to make his way toward the sound of the water. In his mind, the worst-case scenario was that this would be an adventure and he could finally put his emergency kit, which was neatly tucked into his backpack, to the test. He reached the creek and followed it down in elevation until he could see Alouette Lake and its well-established campsites.

Despite being gone longer than anticipated and arriving looking a little worse for wear, with scratches and dirt everywhere, his friends were none the wiser. There were no adults to answer to; this was the group's first independent camping trip. Ron told them confidently that he had just gone on a hike and kept the getting lost part to himself.

Ron didn't need his backpack full of tricks this time, but it was there if he did. He was well ahead of the game, creating buffers between himself and the next adverse event through preparedness. Ron knew what most of us take years to realize: Using the easy times to prepare for the hard times is just good life math.

LIFE ON THE EDGE

NOT-SO-GREAT LIFE MATH IS HOW we often find ourselves living at the margins of our financial means, stress levels, connectedness, and ability to mistreat our own bodies. Sitting at life's cliff-edge, the smallest push can do us in. A flat tire breaks the bank. Prolonged stress becomes illness. A new hurdle, no matter the size, risks becoming unmanageable or compounding into a larger issue because there are no buffers in place to withstand them. It is a reactive life and often an exhausting one.

Living at these edges, in one area or another, happens to the best of us—to most of us. The American Psychological Association's 2023 survey results indicate that top stressors include finances, caregiving, and health. In 2025, Bankrate reported that almost a quarter of Americans have no emergency savings. While one in three people do, it is not enough to cover three months of living expenses.

Loneliness is also prevalent. In 2023, the US Surgeon General's office released an advisory highlighting its significant health risks, which include a 26 percent-increased risk of premature death, a 29 percent-increased risk of heart disease, and a 32 percent-increased risk of stroke. The list goes on.

Instead of contributing to statistics like the ones above, we can build buffers and start living at the limits that set us free—the upper limits of our ability to withstand discomfort, build wealth, increase our health, rethink ideas, learn new skills, and connect with others. Working toward these limits first creates and then reinforces protective buffers against life's adversities, reducing the risk of being pushed over the metaphorical edge of what we can handle.

Take the straightforward outcome of ditching our constant comforts. When we flirt with discomfort regularly, our world expands. If we train in all weather, we can respond in all weather. If we have hard conversations, we can have hard conversations. If we go off on small solo trips, we can build up to bigger independent adventures.

The upper limit of our optimal health is living inside a body that supports the life we want to live. It goes beyond mastering the mundane and dives right into the highest quality of well-being achievable, a level that differs for everyone but offers increased agency for all as optimal health—meaning fewer imposed restrictions due to ill health. This includes increasing fitness potential through capacity rather than aesthetics. Vitality and quality of life are earned here.

The upper limit of financial capacity is about how much more you can save, earn, and invest. The old adage that money can't buy happiness is good-natured and positive. But smart financial moves afford freedom in the form of lifestyle choices, a degree of security, and a greater overall sense of agency.

Living at the upper limit of intellectual curiosity, including the acquisition of skills, means we actively seek knowledge, challenge our assumptions, and pursue the things we have not yet mastered. There is an air of openness to intellectual curiosity that keeps us in growth mode, and building skills makes us less fragile.

The upper limit of connectedness is where we trade false safety for sincerity. It's easy to keep conversations on autopilot: surface-level, safe, and scripted. It's easy to stay home alone, safe with our things. It's easy to not ask for help, even when we need it. Being alone brings a false sense of safety, though. Community is where we thrive. When you want to retreat the most, reach out.

Over time, life at these upper limits becomes familiar.

The upper limits become the desired destination.

They become buffers between you and adversity.

With buffers in place, hurdles become more manageable. This can look like financially floating a year off to transitioning careers after an unexpected job loss, knowing what to do and quickly acting when an extreme weather event occurs, or having a strong enough community to pitch in when you suddenly become ill. All of which I've been through only to be asked later, "How did you manage that?" How I managed is simple. I had robust buffers in place.

BUFFER 1: SECURE

Somewhere along the way, North Americans got really good at two things: not saving for a rainy day and thinking that there should be no rainy days.

We've created an illusion that is bigger than we can afford. The illusion that every adult should own more house than they need, that eating out and fancy lattes are a daily occurrence, and that kids need to be in the best, most expensive programs. Smart phones and new cars for everyone, Botox, massages, and home gyms. What used to be indulgences or extras have now become essentials. There is nothing wrong with any of this unless it's costing you your health, wealth potential, and peace of mind. Then something is definitely off.

We're going to flip the living-up-to-an-illusion script and start by building a financial buffer. Because you can do and have all the things I mentioned above—after you solidify the foundation of having an emergency fund and are debt-free and on track to afford retirement.

There are multiple ways to succeed at building this buffer. You either focus on earning more, saving more, or both. Do it in small annual sprints if that helps, or choose a month and focus on increasing this buffer. Think about the skills, interests, and experiences you have and can leverage. Between skills, stuff, and connections, you already have what you need.

HIGH AGENCY HUMAN

> **SOME WAYS TO EARN EXTRA MONEY INCLUDE** picking up extra shifts at work, preselling a workshop, creating a how-to manual on your expertise and selling it online, offering to pet-sit or dog-walk through pet-sitting sites, listing your home or extra rooms as a vacation or student rental, getting a housemate, selling your home to downsize, bringing clothes to consignment, selling used books through online retailers, selling unused home equipment, renting out your tools and equipment, renting out your backyard and pool for gatherings or as a private dog park, becoming a delivery driver or car sharer, using your truck for dump runs and deliveries, or hosting a garage sale.

WHEN MY HEALTHY SIX-FIGURE CORPORATE contract was unexpectedly cut in 2023, I was a homeowner with 80k in commercial debt, no emergency savings, and, suddenly, no earnings.

The first thing I needed to do was buy myself some time to make longer-term moves, so I signed up to dog-sit for the month, making an average of $600–$800 per week. I was at home figuring out what to do next, so it made sense to earn extra money while doing so. That was an easy $3,000 per month to add to my financial buffer and made me wonder why I wasn't doing something like it once a year or so just to get ahead for a rainy day.

While dog-sitting, I sold household items that I rarely used or were no longer in use, including an extra couch, workout equipment, home decor, and tools. This brought in another $2,600. I sent clothes to the consignment shop and made $325 more. Then I used existing skills to create a website for a friend at the ridiculously low price of six hundred dollars. That brought me to a grand total of $6,525 for the month.

The narrative you tell yourself and others makes or breaks this experience, and I refused to feel embarrassed about boosting my finances by any means necessary. The reality is, these were smart, responsible moves that bought me much-needed time and space to make bigger decisions.

Some ways to save extra money include committing to eating homemade meals during the week, canceling subscriptions and memberships, renegotiating bills, shopping around for better insurance rates, challenging yourself to a no-spend month, carpooling to work or events, switching to no-fee banking and credit cards, trading skills with neighbors and friends, and having your social gatherings at home or outdoors in nature. I ended up saving another four hundred dollars a month by simply canceling and pausing subscriptions and memberships.

During this time, following experts on social media and listening to their podcasts helped me increase my financial literacy and maintain motivation.

Next up was checking organizations and associations I was a member of for available discounts and rates. For you, these might include university alumni associations, trade unions, workplace unions, veterans' groups, community groups, etc. I cut my car and home insurance in half by simply asking if there was a group policy available for categories that might apply to me (e.g., veterans, nurses, or entrepreneurs). This gained me another $630 in savings.

Speaking of insurance, double-check that your policies still fit your lifestyle and goals. After twenty-plus years, I've canceled my life insurance. I'm not saying this is the right move for everyone or that I'll never have life insurance again, but it is the right move for me at this moment since I have no dependents. Instead, I picked up disability insurance and am considering critical illness insurance. You must decide what's best for you. If you have dependents, you might want life insurance. If you're an employee, you may not need disability insurance.

It's worth noting that insurance isn't always the solution you hope it'll be. Major events like the 2024 California wildfires can overwhelm insurance companies and potentially result in underpaid or delayed claims. If all your capital is tied up in your home and related physical assets, it can be hard to survive in the short term as you recover from the loss. Instead, consider speaking to a financial expert, creating a robust long-term plan, and diversifying your assets.

The month I lost my six-figure job, I earned a total of $6,525 and saved $1,030. I should have used my time in a high-paying job to create a financial buffer, and I could have done all these things earlier to accomplish that, but quickly reacting in this way was the second-best-case scenario. The world is chaotic at the best of times; create and diversify your financial buffer so that when the next hurdle comes, you have options and the ability to weather it.

BUFFER 2: STRENGTHEN

SITTING IN THE DOCTOR'S OFFICE, I felt pretty darn pleased with myself. Since my last visit three months ago, I'd managed to reduce my cholesterol levels by 50 percent and lose fifteen pounds to help curb my risk of cardiac disease or an acute event. I was too young to worry about heart attacks, yet here I was.

It started a few years earlier, when lab results seemed to creep out of range for no reason. Of course, there were plenty of reasons: perimenopause, an increasingly sedentary lifestyle, and frequent meals out. But I turned that ship, and by increasing my daily steps to 20,000-plus and losing a little weight, I'd gotten my cholesterol levels into normal range. On the higher side, but still, normal. No statins required, just lifestyle changes. I was still smiling with pride when the doctor walked in with a dose of reality. He reminded me that while I had done well, there was still plenty of work to do. He was rightfully concerned, as my labs from six months prior also showed high ApoB and Lp(a) levels, both indicators of cardiac risk.

Apolipoprotein B (ApoB) is a protein within cholesterol particles; the test measures how many are floating around in the blood. Levels are modifiable with lifestyle changes and, if necessary, medication. We didn't retest for this checkup, so it was likely reduced, but that was no reason to take my foot off the gas and celebrate just yet. The high lipoprotein (a) results and family history of cardiac issues were still an issue. Lp(a) is a non-modifiable genetic risk factor, which makes it all the more important to control modifiable risk factors like cholesterol levels to help mitigate risk.

If I had skipped health appointments and the additional tests, I would have been none the wiser. I would have believed that my current lifestyle was enough and missed the opportunity to increase my health buffer and decrease my risk of cardiac issues.

Don't miss the opportunity to do the same. Consider taking a moment, now or soon, to book any outstanding health-related appointments for the year, like your annual physical, health screenings, and dental exams. Health screenings include (but are not limited to) mammograms, pap smears, colonoscopies, skin checks, etc., as recommended by your physician or local health authority. They are opportunities to discover and address small issues before they become, well, bigger ones. Getting bloodwork while you're healthy, for example, allows you and your healthcare team to establish a baseline to use as a reference down the road if needed or, as in my case, give you enough information to right the ship you didn't realize was headed astray.

Strengthening health includes increasing fitness levels. I've been rucking for years, first with the military, then while building up a local hiking resource business, girlgonegood.com. Rucking is a weight-bearing activity that boosts overall health and well-being. It is a low-impact exercise that strengthens your back and bones, improves posture, and helps build a stronger health buffer. Reading *The Comfort Crisis* by Michael Easter, an author whose insights and adventures have helped further encourage my own, opened the door for me to see rucking as not only a solo endeavor, but also a community-based one through companies like GoRuck. It doesn't have to be rucking; find a physical activity that you enjoy. Rucking is simply my go-to, along with hiking and lifting weights.

BUFFER 3: PREPARE

With the sun shining through the dust-covered windows, I'm sitting in the back seat listening to gritty Pearl Jam tunes while the guys in front immerse themselves in conversation and laughter. I kick the bag on the vehicle floor that I was mocked for overpacking before leaving on this patrol. It is stuffed with garbage bags, supplemental first aid kits, bottles of water, snacks, an extra notepad, warm clothing, a ranger blanket, and glow sticks.

As we approach a curve in the road, I notice that there are dark lumps along the road. No, not lumps. People. People are scattered everywhere. *Where did they all come from? Why is everyone lying down?!* I turn my music off and lean forward, squinting at the scene ahead and trying to make sense of it.

Time slows as we put the pieces together. Minutes earlier, a truck loaded with about fifty passengers lost its brakes and went over the cliff. There are four of us in our vehicle, over thirty people wounded, no medics, and help is hours away. All we have is a satellite phone and my backpack of extras. I can hear nothing but my heartbeat. The situation is now clear. This is a mass casualty event.

Jumping out of our vehicle, we assume control of the scene. After triage, we go down the cliff to help bring up the injured. A little girl dies in my arms. The field ambulances and medevac arrive.

While cleaning up the scene and gathering our things, I notice that we have used every single item I supposedly overpacked: the bottled water to clean wounds prior to dressing, the notepad and sharpie to identify and triage the wounded, the glow sticks to act as a warning to oncoming traffic, and the ranger blanket to warm a person going into shock. Nothing in the first aid kits is left unused. We fill the garbage bags as we clean up the scene. The snacks and clothing warm us as the adrenaline wears off on our drive back. Somewhat miraculously, only two people succumb to injury, one on impact and the little girl. It is a hell of a start to our tour in East Timor. After that, the guys no longer joke about my desire to be ready for anything.

Eventually, scope creep occurred and my preparation went beyond emergency and first aid kits. I started considering what paperwork and plans should I have in place as well.

> **CREATE AND/OR UPDATE YOUR EMERGENCY** kits, plans, and paperwork. This buffer is a pain but worth it. It includes preparing:
>
> - A complete home first aid kit, in an easy-to-access location (make sure to check all the expiration dates)
> - A complete home emergency kit, in an easy-to-access location (make sure to check all the expiration dates)
> - Car emergency and first aid kits, with expiration dates checked, in all vehicles
> - Personal medication and supplements (check the expiration dates)
> - A home fire escape and rendezvous point plan
> - A no-communications and rendezvous point plan
> - Annual home maintenance and safety checks
> - Emergency information sheets (make sure these are all in one location)
> - Updated wills, power of attorney, and advanced care directive forms (or equivalents)
> - In-case-of-death information sheets (completed and shared with your next of kin)
> - Funeral and burial arrangements (or equivalent in accordance with religion and laws)

Taking care of personal affairs in this way, establishing a level of preparedness while you are able and not bogged down with various challenges, is not only a means of caring for loved ones but also a form of self-care. It means that when emergencies arise, you already have the support and contingencies[6] in place to carry you through.

I've had a will and power of attorney in place since 1999. My funeral arrangements have been bought and paid for since 2014. My brother messaged back with a simple "Not funny" when I sent him a picture of myself smiling in front of a tombstone in our national military cemetery. It has my branch insignia, name, rank, service number, and birthdate etched onto it. The only thing missing is the date of death. My brother's response was heartwarming; the kid loves me.

Though death is an often-uncomfortable topic of conversation, having all the arrangements done and paid for leaves me with a sense of calm. Having a weatherproof card in my wallet listing my medical history, current diagnosis if any, medications and supplements, allergies, blood type, contacts, etc. does too. The advanced care directives are up next, and really, I should have done them ages ago. I find that these things don't matter until they do.

---

[6] For additional emergency preparedness resources, visit fema.gov (United States), getprepared.gc.ca (Canada), prepare.campaign.gov.uk (United Kingdom), nema.gov.au (Australia), or civildefence.govt.nz (New Zealand).

AFTER GETTING LOST ON THE camping trip, Ron's interest in preparedness grew beyond emergency and first aid kits. He pursued a career in the military and then became a conservation officer stationed in northern British Columbia, a beautiful and somewhat remote area of Canada that is no stranger to wildfires. The threat looms every spring and becomes a reality each summer. Ron and his wife have grown in their preparedness to evacuate and self-sustain.

"I've lived through wildfires in the community," Ron told me in an interview. "In 2017, a nearby community got their evacuation notice. I was on my way to help, and my wife called to say she could see the fire from the porch and our community hadn't been evacuated yet. I told her to start packing the car with whatever items I listed off the top of my head. She had half an hour to get out of there. Then we were told over the radio that our community was under immediate threat, so I spun around and went back home as fast as I could."

Ron helped his wife evacuate as quickly and safely as possible before returning to work. The state of emergency lasted seventy-seven days, of which Ron worked seventy.

"I saw a lot of families after they were told they had only minutes to get out of their houses or they'd have no time, and the look on their faces—that spinning look of not knowing what to grab. That stuck with me."

When I asked what people normally decide to take in those panicked moments, some of what Ron witnessed surprised me. "Photo albums, pet food, some clothing, and maybe the computer. And then other people grab things like the plastic pool that their dog played in, a basketball, and other stuff that is just not important."

Ron remembers helping another family evacuate. They had young children, so Ron and one of the parents took things like diapers, medications, clothing, and keepsakes. The other parent was outside watering the plants. The moment was so overwhelming and surreal, it was hard to convince them to stop and help with the evacuation.

"A checklist gives you a focus in a time of crisis where you're not panicking, you're going through it and grabbing this and that on the list." A methodical approach to a chaotic moment that you can rely on even when your mind is overwhelmed, checklists give you a sense of control. Ron told me that it is essential to feel in control during a crisis, because things can go sideways the moment you allow yourself to be overwhelmed.

"In 2017, I didn't have a checklist of things I wanted to take, so I told [my wife] all the shit to grab… I had the chance to go back to the house, and I went around and grabbed a couple of emergency items that should've been on the list. I didn't think to tell her, but I thought about them because I physically saw them. We learned a lot from that event."

Two years ago, a forest fire broke out across the street from where Ron and his wife live. And this time, he had a checklist. It was clear and thorough enough that if someone else had been house- or dog-sitting at the time, they would easily have been able to follow it, scoop up the appropriate items, and communicate with Ron in a timely manner. Not only that, his wife walked around and filmed every room before evacuating so they would have a visual record of their belongings in case they eventually needed to submit an insurance claim.

When it comes to creating your own plans and putting together emergency supplies, don't spend where you don't have to. You likely already have everything you need to create a decent emergency kit in your home. You can also create an annual reminder or appointment in your calendar to check all first aid and emergency kits. Discard and replace any expired items, including batteries, medicine, and food. Or you can use the end of daylight saving time in the fall as a prompt to run complete a home maintenance check, update your emergency paperwork if necessary, and review family emergency plans. Try opening the discussion with friends and neighbors; a community is stronger together when they can leverage collective skills, kit, and care.

BUFFER 4: PRACTICE

Snap.

We're an hour from anywhere and about to head out on a ten-mile hike in Gatineau Park, Brandon and Ryan are ready to go, and, while I'm putting on my hiking boots, one of the laces breaks.

HIGH AGENCY HUMAN

"Nooooo," Brandon moans, looking at my boot. "Now what?"

"Oh, don't worry, watch this," Ryan says flatly. I dig through my pack, unzip the emergency kit, and pull out a spare lace.

"You carry spare shoelaces?!" Brandon asks.

"She carries spare *everything*," Ryan replies for me.

The lessons from that mass casualty event in East Timor have never left me. I pack everything, always. And if I have everything, it's best if I know how to use it all and can accurately judge my skills and capabilities.

By mile 10, we realize that we have misjudged the distance. We have lost the trail a few times and are short on water. I have all the gear to address these issues, but gear means little unless you have the skills to use it properly.

Learn and practice a useful skill that adds to your level of preparedness in the wake of an adverse event. What skill would be most useful to you during hard times? What skills do you already have that could be enhanced with practice? What do you wish you could provide for others?

SKILLS TO CONSIDER ACQUIRING AND PRACTICING:

firearms safety • bow hunting • hunting and trapping • fishing • wild plant identification • mushroom identification • map and compass navigation • cold weather survival techniques • fire-starting techniques in all weather conditions • sewing • gardening • basic vehicle maintenance • driving standard transmission vehicles • canning food • cooking meals • treating and filtering safe drinking water • first aid • mental health first aid • wilderness first aid • nonviolent crisis intervention • self-defense • radio communication and antenna theory • generator troubleshooting and maintenance • financial investing • personal cybersecurity • leadership and team management • verbal communication • nonverbal communication • woodworking • basic home maintenance and repairs • shelter-building • financial budgeting • safe food storage.

Find more ideas and recommendations at highagencyhuman.com.

EMERGENCY-PREPAREDNESS COMPANIES ARE ABUNDANT; FEW, however, have products as durable and straightforward to use as Uncharted Supply Co., which launched in 2016 with their signature product, the SEVENTY2® Pro Survival System. I travel with their extremely light triage kit, which I've used in the Arctic and again while hiking in the Pyrenees. Don't ask the founder and CEO Christian Schauf for wild stories of when their products saved the day. The products are so robust and effective, they are often the first line of defense to stop situations from going from bad to worse. Schauf shared with me that "People like to think about big disasters—hurricanes, earthquakes, etc. But the reality is, you're much more likely to have a dead battery, a skinned knee, or be dehydrated. We build products that help navigate both, but my goal is to teach people to practice preparedness in the small moments, and that will prepare them for the bigger moments."

It's not enough to have a spare tire in your car, a glossy new first aid kit, or an emergency communications device; you have to develop your skills and practice using them. Ron echoed this sentiment by stating that we should "practice with the emergency kit. If it can't hold up in practice, it's not going to hold up in a real-life situation."

"Being prepared," Schauf says, "is a constant evolution of skills, gear, and knowledge. If you get complacent, you'll find yourself on the wrong side of that equation." Online searches won't be there to support you when the power grid crashes or you're stuck in the middle of nowhere with no cell reception. To stay functionally prepared, you have to update your first aid training, practice navigation skills, and test any new gear.

It is realistic to practice our skills so we can deal with the outcomes of natural disasters, loss of infrastructure, and the one-offs we just didn't see coming. If the power goes out for days, how and what will you cook? If the car gets a flat tire in the middle of nowhere, can you change it? If there is a vehicle accident, can you positively influence the situation?

LIMITS THAT SET US FREE

A MONTH AFTER LOSING MY government job and working on increasing my financial buffer with small, quick wins, it was time for bigger moves. I sold my house in ten days while the market was good and used the sale to increase my investments by $100,000, create a $20,000 emergency fund, clear what remained of the $80,000 debt, and fund a sabbatical year to focus on a career transition. I downsized into an apartment and sold the extra furniture and items, making an additional $4,000. Thankfully I was sitting on a degree in nursing, which allowed me to take the registered nurse license exam and start a new career in an in-demand field.

With my financial buffer bumped up, I ended up taking a dream trip to the Arctic, followed by Finland, hiking in Andorra, and, finally, participating in a GoRuck event for the eightieth anniversary of D-Day in Normandy, France. I rucked more that day than I thought I possibly could, after signing up for a fifteen-kilometer ruck that turned out to be a fifteen-*mile* event that turned out to be *more* than fifteen miles. I found it challenging and decided to come home and start my own rucking routine with a friend to further build that health buffer. The bigger these buffers become, and the more I operate at my upper limits, the freer I feel to experience life.

There is no need to focus on building buffers all year long. Just bump them up as needed.

CHAPTER 7

Pursue Peak Conditioning

The purpose of training is to tighten up the slack, toughen the body, and polish the spirit.
—Morihei Ueshiba

"Is that how you welcome all the new jumpers?" I mustered just enough ego to spew this at the infantry officer with a half-smile before walking past the entire jump company and around the corner of the hangar. Out of sight of the others, I bent over, braced myself against the cold metal siding, and started to hyperventilate while fighting back the urge to cry. My body needed to release a mixture of adrenaline and fear.

The hangar and drop zone were on base, and I was attached to an infantry battalion as my last posting before release. It seemed full circle to end my career at the same military base it started with, no longer the young kid who got her face smashed in by a tank but now an experienced skydiver. While the company was there prepping for a static jump, I had just finished freefalling from a helicopter with some of the men in the recce platoon. Normally, my ego loved freefalling and showing off some skills. The only thing I proved that day, though, is that shit happens and training works.

With more than five hundred jumps and both military and civilian qualifications, I had spent hours upon hours going over skydiving emergency drills in my head and visualizing exactly how I would respond to each possible variation of emergency, often practicing the movements physically while playing out the scenarios in my mind.

As soon as I jumped out of the helicopter and pulled the pilot chute that day, I knew something was off. Instead of looking up at a beautiful canopy slowly unfurling into steady fullness, I saw the lines twisted all the way up and over the crumpled canopy, which was flapping like a garbage bag in the wind. First issue, the line twists. Second issue, lines over.

While I tried kicking myself out of the line twists and keeping an eye on altitude, I rattled off the options in my head. If I couldn't make the canopy flyable by a certain altitude, I'd have to cut away and deploy the reserve. It was a military parachute, we were jumping without equipment at lower altitude, and I only weighed a buck fifty. I had it in my head that not wing-loading the parachute meant a slower opening, and this was already taking too long to fix. The altimeter on my wrist showed 1,500 feet when the mess of a canopy dipped from above me to the same level and started to spin. Well, that was emergency issue number three. *To hell with this.* I released my junk parachute and deployed the emergency reserve. In the first milliseconds, it felt like I was Wile E. Coyote falling through the air with time standing still before the white canopy appeared, stabilized, and I was back in control.

Adversity is often the gut punch we weren't expecting and, as legendary basketball all-star and coach Steve Nash said, "You have to rely on your preparation. You got to really be passionate and try to prepare more than anyone else, and put yourself in a position to succeed, and when the moment comes you got to enjoy, relax, breathe and rely on your preparation so that you can perform and not be anxious or filled with doubt." I didn't plan to cut away my parachute that day, but I was ready for it.

Preparedness gives us the upper hand and some breathing room to stop things from getting worse. Contingency plans, practiced skills, mental rehearsals, and purposeful and gradual exposure to stressors have helped me ride adversity waves over the years.

DIRT DIVES ON REPEAT

LIKE MOST KIDS, MY IMAGINATION was an escape. I'd curl up in a warm blanket on a cool night to immerse myself in the world of the Hardy Boys or Nancy Drew, imagining what their adventures would be like and playing out scenarios in my mind to "solve the case." By the time I joined the military, that imagination had expanded to include emergency scenarios—no books required, just me escaping to an imaginary world and going over them again and again and again. The building is on fire; what should I do first? There's a multi-vehicle crash; how do I control the scene? I would mentally exhaust all options and all possible outcomes.

My favorite time to let my mind wander into these scenarios was while running. I'll swear up, down, and sideways that it helped increase my run times. It also left me feeling more capable. But was I?

It wasn't until I started skydiving that the term "dirt dive" came into play and brought my mental imagery game up a notch. It is used to describe the physical practice of the skydiving sequence on the ground. When done solo, it often involves visualization. It's quite normal to see a skydiver intently focused or with their eyes shut, going over their skydiving sequence while physically recreating it with micro-movements. If this happened anywhere but a drop zone, you might think they had lost their marbles. This type of practice not only increases proficiency in the sport, it is also used to practice emergency scenarios and create muscle memory. It added a kinesthetic component to a visualization practice I had already established.

These mental scenarios were vivid. They allowed me to practice calm through moments of chaos, a kind of meditation. Also, not unlike being a player in my own video game, they allowed me to practice reactions A, B, and C to scenario one over and over while figuring out which avenue was the best case and what to do in the worst case.

When I had the skydiving emergency that day in front of the whole battalion, the only scenario I hadn't previously played out in my mind was retrieving the main canopy. I never followed the cutaway main parachute to get it like we're supposed to do. While perhaps annoying for the gents who had to go find it in the woods, it didn't impact anyone's safety. Plus, now we had something to joke about, the oh-so-experienced jumper forgetting a drill.

Mental rehearsals with the physical component of micro-movements aren't just for skydivers; pilots and surgeons use the same tool. Pilots call it "chair flying" (I like the grittiness of "dirt diving" better), and over 90 percent of surgeons practice this technique before stepping into the operating room. This type of rehearsal builds familiarity with procedures and different scenarios, reduces cognitive load in real time, and helps skydivers, pilots, and surgeons anticipate and appropriately react to the unexpected. It works.

I remember going for a skydive at my local drop zone. Besides the pilot, it was just me and my friend Tim, both of us relaxing (read: napping) in the back of the Cessna on the climb to altitude. It was a beautifully warm, sunny day, and the hum of the plane felt like a lullaby. The stall alarm woke us. The pilot tensed and started working the problem. The alarm didn't cease. The pilot calmly but firmly yelled the emergency procedure words "Get. Out. Now."

Tim and I checked the altitude, opened the door, visually scanned the sky, and jumped out before the pilot finished enunciating the "ow" in "now." We had years of practice and mental rehearsal of emergency drills, and could anticipate and appropriately react to the unexpected. We landed safely at the edge of the drop zone, and the pilot made an emergency landing in a nearby farmer's field.

The act of mental rehearsal creates neural pathways, similar to experiencing an event in real life, and boosts reaction time, confidence, and calm under pressure. To improve outcomes, this technique can be applied to preparing for emergency scenarios as much as for stressful everyday events. You can use mental rehearsal to prepare for natural disasters, infrastructure breakdown, and accidents, or the next meeting you need to lead, race you are running, or task you need to accomplish. To apply this technique, use vivid, structured visualization before a known stress event and pair it with micro-movements to engage kinesthetic memory. Imagine the scenario step by step and repeatedly visualize a perfect performance, or introduce disruptions and rehearse how to respond to them. Let this be a place where you can troubleshoot possible actions and outcomes in a safe and controlled manner. Make sure you control the show when visualizing emergency scenarios instead of letting unsolicited negative ruminations take over.

Like everything else in this book, I'm sharing what I've learned over time and works for me. You get to choose what to adapt and what to ditch.

FULL DRESS REHEARSALS

It was a bright, clear day. I was playing cards at the picnic table, enjoying the view of rugged alpine peaks all around us, when our easygoing day was broken by a loud whizzing sound followed by a thick plume of smoke, a blaze, and the scream of the camp's emergency siren.

I was eighteen and working at a cadet camp in the Canadian Rockies when a Cessna plane crashed in our compound and immediately caught fire. Staff and cadets alike, one of whom was Ron, were putting out the fire and providing first aid. By this time, Ron had already joined the military and was much further ahead in skill and preparedness. Someone called 911. I helped clear the sleeping quarters and direct kids to our safety point. Others gathered in their respective areas and counted heads. Imagine a compound with hundreds of kids and only a few adults to act quickly and decisively in response to an emergency.

Most everyone had first aid and leadership training, and we had all practiced fire drills. When the plane crashed, we fell into place and performed our roles. This event became a building block of my approach to future emergencies and adverse events.

Repetition of movement works to reduce the cognitive load during an event; you end up acting without thinking much about what you're doing. Your body already knows. Whether it's conducting fire drills with the family, lifting heavy things outdoors to improve functional fitness, or running through first aid scenarios, keep practicing.

Physical rehearsal also allows you to quickly find out if part of your plan doesn't work in application. Exiting the building through the window during a fire is great in theory, but have you practiced opening it? Moving through it? Have you taken the emergency escape ladder out of the packaging and tested it? We already do physical rehearsals with fire drills at schools and CPR compression during first aid classes—why not expand to other areas, like home emergencies or exercising in varied weather to forge resilience and capability?

Physical rehearsal can also be a means of shifting our mental perspective. As Nicolette Sawder, founder of Wilder Child, wrote, "Practice going outside in *all* weather. It builds resilience but more importantly it saves you from spending your life merely tolerating the 'bad' days in favor of a handful of 'good' ones… a life of endless expectations and conditions where happiness hinges on sunshine." What a shift to practice to such a degree and become capable in all conditions, like the well-weathered humans we are meant to be.

EXERCISE STRESS THRESHOLD

Are they nuts? That can't be comfortable. Why aren't they sheltered, where it's warmer? I would be. I am. Sitting in my parked car with a toque and winter jacket on, I run the car every so often so that the warm air and heated seats can soak through my layers. It's 32°F outside. Not the worst, but there is a wet chill about the day that goes right to the bones. In front of me, the waves of Lake Huron crash against the rocky shoreline. The water looks dark and uninviting. Yet the seagulls and ducks on the water are completely unbothered, whitecaps and weather be damned. A relaxed little group on the waves, occasionally bobbing for fish. Snow starts to litter the skies and I pull the collar of my sweater up around my neck. Deep down, I envy the birds' calm resilience.

Staying comfortable is risky behavior. Purposefully immersing in and exposing ourselves to stressful experiences is smart conditioning.

Exercising our stress response can help increase our adaptability to future stressful events. In his book *What Happened to You?*, Dr. Bruce Perry states that "Predictable, controllable, and moderate activation of the stress-response system has been shown to build our capacity to manage challenges… It's the dose, the pattern, and the controllability that determine whether the stress is adaptive or harmful." On the flip side, "The more our stress-response system is activated in uncontrollable ways, the less able we are to handle even small amounts of stress." The good news is, we can take control of conditioning our stress response to avoid the latter scenario. The key, of course, is to purposely expose ourselves to stress in the right environment and at a duration and intensity that promote growth.

The practical application is to introduce low-dose, controlled stress activities in safe, graded steps: a few seconds of cold water gradually building up to a cold shower, run-walk cycles building up to running a desired distance, speaking up in small meetings before presenting to a large audience, exercising outdoors in all weather before embarking on a multi-day adventure.

You can take it a step further and do something I like to call a comfort fast: deliberate removal of modern conveniences, small luxuries, and ease for a set period to rebuild your tolerance for adversity. The Stoics called it "voluntary discomfort." Modern science calls it "hormesis" (an adaptive response to moderate stress). In *The Comfort Crisis*, author Michael Easter brings the Japanese term *misogi* to our attention, a traditional practice of washing the body in cold water to promote personal growth through mental and physical challenge. Our modern world has broadened the meaning. While the end goal remains personal growth, *misogi* is now seen as any endeavor that challenges us physically and psychologically. Whatever you call it—comfort fast, voluntary discomfort, hormesis, or *misogi*—the effect is the same: You build strength through chosen struggle so you can better face unknown adversities down the road. Just make sure to consider taking Dr. Perry's advice before tackling your next challenge by making it short, safe, and low-dose.

As I sat in my car, it seemed like the seagulls were mocking me with their apparent ease and disregard for the weather. *This is ridiculous.* I got out of the car, stripped down to the bathing suit I was wearing under all those layers, took a few deep breaths, and walked into the water. I looked at the birds, then up at the falling snow. The cold breath of nature wasn't going to stop me, and knowing that felt better than any discomfort I experienced in the moment.

Studies suggest that stress, when perceived as a challenge rather than a threat, can actually enhance performance and resilience. In a 2013 study published in *Health Psychology*, researchers found that individuals who viewed stress as a natural, enhancing response were less likely to suffer adverse health effects than those who saw it as harmful. What does this tell us? The way we perceive and respond to stress matters just as much, if not more, than the fact that stress is present. We can manage the impact of stress by managing our perception of and response to it.

DISCOVER YOUR MORAL ARCS

IMAGINE THAT THERE IS A mass shooting and you're the only uninjured person on the scene. You have one personal first aid kit on you. There are two young kids with equally life-threatening injuries. Which kid do you help first?

Now imagine that your unexpected physiological response is to freeze. You are incapable of moving and a kid's health starts to decline. How do you come to terms with your reaction? Or perhaps you are the medic in this scenario, ordered to help Kid A instead of Kid B even though your instinct is the opposite, and Kid B succumbs to injury. How, if at all, do you resolve going against your better judgment?

This event might sound extreme, yet whether it's Mother Nature or a bad actor in society, adverse events like mass casualty incidents (MCIs) are now a common occurrence in North America. MCIs are ripe breeding grounds for moral injury. A moral injury is a distressing result of participating in or witnessing an event comprised of behaviors that contrast with our values or moral beliefs. It juggles what we personally perceive as right or wrong in a situation when there is a dissonance between the event and our personal action (or inaction). While the term is fairly well known within military and emergency response communities, they are not the only susceptible populations. In 2025, moral injury received long-overdue official recognition by the American Psychiatric Association and was included in *The Diagnostic and Statistical Manual of Mental Disorders* (DSM) used by American healthcare providers.

The risk of moral injury can arise around the sensitive and very personal dilemma of whether or not to have an abortion. Journalists who cover humanitarian crises or natural disasters can be weighed down by moral decisions. Knowing who you are and having that strong sense of identity along with clear personal values can help you navigate muddled situations that risk moral injury.

Moral injuries can haunt you for a moment, a season, or a lifetime. If you want to avoid or at least have a fighting chance of processing this type of situation, it might help to be proactive by figuring out your moral arcs. Understanding them will assist with decision-making in the moment; they are the limits of what you can and cannot live with.

In Afghanistan, the risk of moral injury came in the form of an old man pushing a wheelbarrow through the desert heat, over hard terrain, in chewed-up flip-flops.

"Wicky, you need to come to the front gate." I looked up from my desk to see a wide-eyed Saad with the corporal behind him. I got up, grabbed my weapon and flak vest, and followed them out to the gate.

What I found was an old man with his wheelbarrow. Normally, we got people in who were requesting financial compensation for the destruction of property or crops from recent fighting we were involved in. But this wasn't that and something was off. Toes from two little bare feet peeked over the rim of the wheelbarrow and the full picture came into frame. This man, older and quite frail, had walked miles with the child in the wheelbarrow for medical attention. As the man pointed at the child's abdomen, I cautiously lift the soiled and torn T-shirt to reveal a layers-deep, four-inch-long laceration. It was infected; the child was both feverish and nauseous. I smiled at the child before seeing if the medics would take him.

The response over the radio was gutting: "Negative, we are unable to intake the child."

One thing I do not have is a good poker face. I had no idea how many miles it was to the nearest NGO for aid, but

I knew that between the distance, the unforgiving terrain, the man's fragility, and the infection oozing from the child's stomach, there was no win here.

This moment was ripe for moral injury. Weighing all possible actions and outcomes was crucial. It all boiled down to one primary question: Not what the child needed. Not what the old man wanted. Not what I was ordered to do. But what could I live with? What possible action in this scenario would pose the least risk of my developing a moral injury? What action would maintain or least challenge my core values?

I lifted the child's T-shirt and cleaned the wound with my own supplies while explaining what I was doing to the grandfather through the interpreter. The child endured the cleaning and bandaging with only a few quiet tears from his big brown eyes that reminded me, for a split second, of the kid who had died in East Timor years before. Then I gave him a toy, cookies, and a bottle of water, and the grandfather a few first aid supplies. The grandfather offered gratitude, grasped the wheelbarrow handles, and walked away.

It was the most I could do, the least I could live with, and the right decision in accordance with my personal values to avoid a moral injury. The decision was tough, but having a clear understanding of my moral arcs made it easier.

An exercise I use to help uncover moral arcs is what skydivers call "dirt diving." It's the visualization technique I discussed earlier, in which you go through entire scenarios, injecting different possibilities and playing out each outcome. While you're doing this type of visualization exercise using emergency scenarios, take note of how you feel and use that as a cue to drive you to recognition of your moral arcs. You can talk it out with mentors, therapists, or spiritual advisors.

The next adversity will come, whether we signed up for it or not. Most of us aren't great at training for a challenge until after it has arisen; we suffer, then realize the value of being better prepared. We can learn instead to embrace the discomfort of now to facilitate our ability to manage tomorrow. We can use visualization, physical rehearsal, and chosen discomfort to meet life at the level where it's going to hit us.

CHAPTER 8

Switch Off Autopilot

You have to assemble your life yourself, action by action.
—Marcus Aurelius

THREE CLOSE FRIENDS SIT AROUND a kitchen island. Well, two of us are seated. The other one is half out of her seat, her voice raised and her hands enunciating every syllable.

Bonnie pipes up during a pause. "Wait, did you say your friend is taking a GLP-1 and not weight training?"

"Yah, and complaining about muscle loss," Trish continues. "Every doctor I've heard talk about this mentions that weight training is important, otherwise you risk losing muscle tone and bone density. I even offered to go over and help them start a basic weightlifting routine. I'd happily do that. It's been months. Nothing. The opportunity is right there. It's frustrating."

"I can imagine. I know you care," says Bonnie, leaning in. "Oh hey, did you read anything more on brain health benefits from creatine?"

"Yep, I just finished listening to another podcast on that and was about to look up the research. Hold on, I'll send you the link." Trish grabs her phone and sends the info to our group chat.

Although the conversation ping-pongs quite a bit, I'm appreciating that this is the type of chat we have on a near-weekly basis. I can't help but smile, take another sip of coffee, and join in.

"I wonder if I should adjust the amount I'm taking…" I say without really needing an answer. "Oh, did you hear that a ketamine clinic popped up the next town over?"

Bonnie tilts her head slightly. "It's starting to gain traction. But does it really work? Or are we creating more issues?"

"I mean, maybe both?" I put down my coffee mug. "There's a lot of newer research on benefits as long as there's appropriate intervention and follow-up. I think that's the key. I spoke to a neurosurgeon last week and had a fascinating conversation on neural pathways. Everything from anxiety to stroke to everyday thinking and behaviors. I'm interested to see where more trials in research lead with psychedelic-assisted psychotherapy."

We spend the next twenty minutes discussing what we know about the brain and how we can use that knowledge to reach our own health goals. We discuss, debate, and, perhaps most importantly, question insights we've gained from books, research papers, and expert interviews on podcasts. Our trio's curiosity about all things health-related, and how to apply that knowledge to our everyday lives, seems endless.

"How can anyone not be obsessed with how their brain and body work?!?" Trish asks.

"It's fascinating," I say.

"And damn useful," Bonnie concludes.

Useful is an understatement. We must understand the brain, and our physiological workings as a whole, as a matter of increasing agency. That understanding allows us to put more votes towards the outcomes we desire. We can make informed lifestyle choices, adjust our fitness routines, and work collaboratively with healthcare professionals to increase our vitality.

If you know that hearing loss is a risk factor for dementia, for example, you can choose a career that limits your exposure to loud noise, wear earplugs at concerts, and get regular testing.

If you know that loneliness corresponds to higher health risks than smoking, you can start to build deep, long-lasting friendships or move to a more community-minded town.

If you know that a lack of mobility is linked to decreased quality of life in aging, you can hire a trainer to help you build bone and muscle strength now.

As in much of this book, I'm talking about a proactive approach that provides a level of comfort from knowing that we're doing what we can, when we can. Without that, we risk living on autopilot—an obvious analogy for operating subconsciously, without pausing to reflect and readjust.

HIGH AGENCY HUMAN

To be fair, autopilot has its merits. Think of those subconscious decisions that benefit you either in the form of a healthy habit, like brushing your teeth in the morning, or by lightening the cognitive load, like when you drive to work but still have the bandwidth to hold a conversation or listen to a podcast. How many times have you been chatting with friends while driving and then thought, *Oh shit, we're here?* You have years of driving under your belt and autopilot, your subconscious, took care of stopping at lights, turning right, and slowing down for you while you laughed and argued good-naturedly with your passengers. Of course it goes beyond this classic example; think of automatic responses during social interactions, brewing your coffee in the morning, or taking the same running route every day. Tasks done without thinking free our minds for other thoughts. Autopilot can be handy and efficient.

It's the other side of autopilot, where life becomes automatic in ways that are unfulfilling or even detrimental, that we're going to disrupt, switch off, by leveraging how our body works and our brain's neuroplasticity. High agency is found in awareness and action. Instead of living on autopilot and moving through the day to day without leveraging knowledge that is available to us all, we will gather around the metaphorical kitchen island with curiosity—first to gain a basic understanding of our physiological workings, then to embrace the continuous cycle of discussion, learning, and rethinking.

The degree to which you have a say over your future body and mind is determined by the actions you take today. Later is a now problem.

Disease is created over time, but so are strength and health. Each action is a vote whose consequences you tend not to see until your votes compound over time. And the most interesting aspect of increasing agency through understanding our inner workings—at least in my opinion—lies in harnessing the power of the mind.

MAPPING THE MIND

You're hiking in the woods on a well-managed trail. There are signs every fifty yards and trail system maps at every intersection. The path is well-worn, wide, and on relatively flat terrain. It's ridiculously easy to navigate, so easy that you hike it every morning without thinking twice. You know that just past the large stump, there's a short uphill grade, and once at the pond there is only another quarter mile or so until the lookout. It's a familiar, comfortable hike.

It's not the only lookout in the area, though there is no trail to the second spot; you have to break one. A week later, you've bought new hiking boots, taken an orienteering refresher course, and listened to your favorite tunes while driving back out to the trailhead.

First, you need to clear a route, cut down shrubs, and remove large trip hazards. This takes multiple visits. Once you've made something resembling a trail, you construct and place directional signs so you don't get turned around. In the midst of your sweaty efforts, you're put off by swarms of mosquitoes and black flies.

The days seem to go on forever. It's hard, uncomfortable work. It would be easier to quit and go back to taking the established trail you used to hike daily, to the lookout point you know so well. With each visit, you dismiss the urge and persist through the discomfort, but not without some grumbles and setbacks. Eventually, you look up and think, *Oh hey now, this is starting to look like a halfway decent trail*. You hike it a few times a day at the beginning, until it's truly clear. Then you start to enjoy it and take pride in it. The new lookout is spectacular; you can't believe you haven't cleared a path to it earlier. Barring a natural disaster, this solid, clear path is here to stay, along with your access to incredible views.

Existing trails and creating new trails are how I like to think about neural pathways, neural circuits, and neuroplasticity, respectively. A neural pathway is a trail that connects neurons and sends information along its route. A neural circuit is similar to a neural pathway, but more complex; think of a trail system instead of a single trail. Like the number of stars in the galaxy, the neuron count in the brain changes as our understanding grows; suffice to say, it is in the billions. Billions of neurons and who knows how many possible routes and configurations.

It helps to mull these concepts with someone who understands them fully, so I got in touch with Dr. D.J. Cook, neurosurgeon and chief medical officer for Dimensions, an organization I've come to appreciate for its informed and considerate approach to veteran health. When a doctor takes that small rubber hammer and taps just under your knee, resulting in your lower leg reflexively jerking upward, that is an example of myotatic reflex circuitry, in which the connections are "one neuron that transmits an action potential to the spinal cord, synapses to an interneuron and a motor neuron, and transmits an action potential back to muscle spindles that fire and trigger the reflex." Dr. Cook explains. There are multiple neural pathways in a circuit to perform a specific task; in this case, the reflex of the lower leg jerking upward and then relaxing again. In our hiking analogy, think of a circuit as multiple trails within in a trail system that connect to lead you to a specific lookout before continuing the loop back toward the trailhead.

Some regions of the brain are focused on managing one specific output, like our motor output example above. Then we have other regions that are much more complex and interconnected, "like the parietal lobe," Dr. Cook continues, "which is a transmodal area, an integration center. It takes sensory, motor, and cognitive information, processes these, modifies as needed, and creates a new output." Neural pathways, circuits, and the interconnectedness of the nervous system are a lot to take in, and there is so much we don't yet know, but think of the brain and body as being filled with established hiking trails (neural pathways) and trail systems (neural circuits) through diverse terrain (different brain areas) connecting trailheads to lookouts (behaviors, physical movement, etc.).

INTENTIONAL DISRUPTION

OUR BRAINS ARE MALLEABLE. We can form new neural connections throughout life. This means that no matter how deeply ingrained our habits or thought patterns may be, we have the capacity to change, grow, and adapt to whatever life throws at us. The work of Dr. Norman Doidge, author of *The Brain That Changes Itself*, demonstrates that people have rewired their brains to overcome strokes, trauma, and even chronic pain. Our very biology is built to adapt.

To create a new path, we first need to understand the foundation that is neuroplasticity. Dr. Cook explained to me that the "overall concept is that the brain is able to make changes on a cellular and ultimately, network basis, to create new connectivity patterns that drive a behavior." Neuroplasticity, and how we engage with it, is important as it impacts our adaptability, memory and cognitive function, and ability to heal and recover. In short, it determines our human experience and level of resilience.

Interventions that promote neuroplasticity include repeated activities like exercise, mindfulness, and medication (anesthetics like ketamine and psychedelics like psilocybin), and magnetic and electrical stimulation treatments. It will be interesting to see where the research with these treatments leads. Cognitive behavioral therapy

(CBT) and eye movement desensitization and reprocessing (EMDR) also work by reinforcing and accessing neuroplasticity. All of these interventions require licensed professionals to administer and guide them to ensure safety and adaptive outcomes. There is plenty we can do ourselves, however. We can master the basics from chapter 4 (nutrition, physical activity, stress management, social connection, and avoiding risky substance use), practice metacognition (self-reflection, journaling, meditation, mindfulness, and therapy) and yoga, and engage in new and novel experiences (like learning a new language or skill, traveling to a new location, or taking a different route home). I mean really, if you needed an excuse to finally take that trip, here it is.

These interventions are often described as rewiring the brain, a process that requires certain conditions and components: a degree of focus or a high emotional need for change; the presence of neuromodulators like epinephrine, norepinephrine, acetylcholine, or dopamine (to create a neuroplastic state through the actions mentioned above); and professional guidance such as psychotherapy, self-directed thought exercises, or intentional action as intervention.

The part we often miss, in today's overstimulating world, is allowing space for reflection after the intervention and then following that up with a good night's sleep. It's too easy to turn on the radio, scroll social media, or listen to a podcast on the drive home after treatment, but really, we should abstain from extra noise and sit with what we just experienced, giving those neural pathways the opportunity to reinforce themselves. Dr. Cook explains that "The critical steps in achieving a good therapeutic outcome are—to use words from the psychedelic world—you have to start with an intention, follow with the intervention, and then you carry on with appropriate integration to reinforce and cement the desired change." He reminds us that having the intention to change and a deep desire *for* change matters. "A person has to want to engage in the therapy, they have to agree that there are some maladaptive aspects to the way they're thinking or the way they're experiencing the world or their emotional state, in order to [take the next] step with change." After these components for change are implemented, it's on to repetition, repetition, repetition.

UNWANTED MANIPULATORS

NOT ALL REWIRING IS INTENTIONAL. You can create the most beautiful trail to enjoy, hike it daily for years, and Mother Nature can destroy it all with a single weather event. Life works in much the same way; unexpected events or unexamined exposure can leave us with unwanted changes to our neural pathways. Some of the more common examples include traumatic brain injuries (TBIs) or concussions, which can result in a dysfunction in neurovascular coupling (a.k.a. the relationship between the neurons and the blood vessels that supply oxygen and nutrients to them), with the neurons either getting too little or too much oxygen.

Then there are viral and bacterial infections, such as HSV-1, influenza, long COVID, and Lyme disease, that can result in neuroinflammation—neuron damage or cell death. Research into the neural impact of infections is complex and relatively new, but it does indicate that such infections have resulted in new onset symptoms like depression or anxiety.

Strokes, an area of expertise for Dr. Cook, are caused by a lack of oxygen and nutrients supplied to the neurons, resulting in neural death. "In stroke," he says, "we're trying to fix a modal region of the brain, like the primary motor cortex. We're trying to remap it to a different part of the brain so that [the patient can, for example] start moving their hand again."

With seizures, the resulting rewiring can have an effect I found surprising. Dr. Cook gives the classic example of having a tumor in your left temporal lobe that irritates the hippocampus. Then "what happens is that you have a seizure in your left temporal lobe. The way seizures work is, they spread over the rest of the brain. What can happen eventually, with time and chronic exposure, is you develop seizure after seizure, generating circuitry in the opposite side of the brain because there's neuroplasticity within the amygdala and hippocampus, that respond to these repeated events by developing a new epileptogenic focus—which can then generate seizures from the other side, termed kindling. That's an example of neuroplasticity" (though not the kind of neuroplasticity we're after).

Finally, such rewiring can happen as a result of trauma, such as the physical trauma of being shot or developing post-traumatic stress disorder (PTSD).

We would not choose to experience any of these things, but we can choose how to recover from them. Treatments vary greatly, yet the components remain the mostly the same: a degree of focus or a strong emotional desire for change, neuroplasticity, intervention, reflection, sleep, and repetition.

ADDITIONAL ACTS OF AGENCY

THE PREFRONTAL CORTEX IS FOR decision-making, cortisol is a stress hormone, and anxiety is a psychological issue. This is an easy and organized way to think about our bodies, yet we know that it's more complex and intertwined than that. The prefrontal cortex plays a role in emotional regulation, self-reflection, and planning. The medial prefrontal cortex is part of the default mode network (DMN), a resting state network that is active when you're driving to work while daydreaming about an upcoming trip or taking a walk at lunch and ruminating on a comment made by a coworker. Cortisol regulates metabolism, mediates inflammatory responses, and can help control your heart rate and blood pressure. Anxiety can have physiological origins.

The cells and systems in our bodies work in conjunction with each other and with cascading effects. They are not separate entities to analyze, support, or treat. We can see this perspective gaining acceptance within emerging fields like psychoneuroimmunology, the study of the changes in immune function influenced by the relationship between our endocrine (hormonal) and nervous (thinking/behavior) systems. It's the understanding, for example, that a rash could be an allergic or stress-related reaction. One can be healed with medication and the other with therapy.

We tend to think of our ability to heal from wounds as a purely physical endeavor, but what about the effects of our psychological state on the time it takes to heal? Stressful social interactions can alter the skin's ability to heal, with one study by Drs. Kiecolt-Glaser, Loving, and Stowell demonstrating that couples "who demonstrated consistently higher levels of hostile behaviors across… their interactions healed at 60% of the rate of low-hostile couples." Who we heal around affects how we heal. Interesting, right? It is also actionable. You can use this level of understanding to help in your own healing and the recovery of loved ones.

If we compartmentalized all of our bodily systems and created a Venn diagram of their influence and impact, we would see an overwhelming number of shaded areas indicating overlap. There is often more influencing our health and psychological states than we assume, and we can increase our agency by becoming critically curious and open to solutions that we may not previously have considered. The more we know, the more we can consider and act on.

CHAPTER 9

High Agency Human

Life is like a game of cards. The hand you are dealt is determinism; the way you play it is free will.

—Jawaharlal Nehru

"It's good to see you never lost your courage."

The handwritten words and signature stare back at me from the piece of paper in my hands. It was torn from a notepad, the kind you tuck into a shirt pocket; the paper is crisp and the ink vivid. It could have been written yesterday. But these words, this signature—it just couldn't be.

I toss around the few old letters and mementos in the fire safe, looking for more evidence. Nothing. Nothing else from this time or person. Just this note.

Its writer, Matt, is a good friend, a solid man known for his kindness. His note is an apology for not staying more closely connected over the years, and to say that even though we haven't been in touch, he's been cheering me on from a distance. This is what brotherhood in the military, and in life, means to me. We're not always close, but there for each other to weather hard times or celebrate success.

Matt was passing though base while we were both deployed in Afghanistan and left the note on my bunk. We missed seeing each other in person, and on the next deployment, he died.

That was twenty years ago.

His words were found and resonated today.

Because I have, in fact, lost my courage.

At least that's what this feels like. A defeat. A giving in. A cowardly acceptance. I was sick with a virus a few months ago and it began instantly—relentless and debilitating waves of anxiety attacks, two or three a day. The nausea, perhaps the thing I loathe most, lasts four to six hours with each attack. Then there are the darker thoughts that seem real even when I know they are not. It feels like a weighted blanket is wrapped around my mind and the smallest of missteps, like eating or stress, sets off the next wave of misery. Wave upon wave upon wave. I fear it. I've given in to it. I'm in the middle of an anxiety attack right now. There's no rhyme or reason behind it, it's just here. Sorting through my things was meant as a distraction, and then I found the note.

The coolness of the hardwood floor in my apartment feels good, a momentary sense of relief. I look at Matt's words, then at my military medals and my grandmother's pearls, also in the safe: all reminders of agency, capability, and grit. Matt always made life happen, the medals are symbols of my own ability to live big, and my grandmother, well, she was the very definition of grit. Another wave of nausea is incoming and the heat rises up through my body. I want to turtle and ignore the world until it goes away, but I think my incredibly wise friend Lynne was right yesterday when she matter-of-factly stated that I might be the main contributor to this purgatorial state.

I want to be the person Matt knew. The one with courage, and a lot of gumption. And if I want to be that person, I have to *be* that person.

It's time to get up off the floor and get to work.

I'VE LOST COUNT OF THE times I've been told that experiencing anxiety attacks will be a lifelong struggle, something to accept, something unchangeable, by friends, colleagues, and doctors alike. And maybe that's what they know, the experience they've had. But I know and you know that when we operate as High Agency Humans, most things are changeable or, at minimum, within our grasp to influence in our favor. We have an influencing role in our outcomes and the agency to switch gears when we need to. Anxiety attacks are not a label nor an identity, but an experience to move through. This is simply the next obstacle in this season's hero's journey in a life full of hero's journeys.

In the few months after I discovered Matt's note, it took applying everything I knew—everything you now know too—to create change. I immediately pulled the emergency brake with a reduction in almost all areas. I left my nursing job on good terms. Some thought I was crazy to leave a relatively new job, but it didn't matter. I knew that I needed to pull back to move forward. Thankfully, I had used the good times before this to prepare for the hard times and created a financial buffer I could lean on while figuring out my health. I stopped writing, stopped socializing, and started eating simple meals. I slept a lot. Life was reduced to only the absolute necessities.

During the next three months, I stayed in that reduced state while trying to understand not only what I was going through, but how exactly to move through it. I gladly accepted help from medical professionals and leaned on family and friends, sleeping over on nights when I wasn't feeling the best. Breathing exercises, meditation, hours of playing simple online games—I did anything I could to create a steadier state of being and a little space to work on myself. When that space came, when the anxiety attacks went from a few daily to every few days, I was able to push forward. Instead of being driven by anxiety, I switched off autopilot by speaking to others with similar experiences, and doctors, therapists, and neurosurgeons, gathering as much insight on how the brain works and coping mechanisms as possible. I consumed articles, books, and podcasts on neurology, psychology, and metabolic health, and then applied that knowledge, testing out what worked and didn't work for me. I pursued peak conditioning through visualization at night and exercising my stress threshold during the day. This meant doing what I didn't feel like doing but knew was good for me, like social gatherings, exercise, and going outside, in small doses that I gradually increased. I started purposely increasing my heart rate by walking fast, then focused on keeping my mind calm. My conscious, intentional, and persistent efforts mirrored different aspects of this book. Nothing was linear, and these efforts often overlapped.

There were some wins and a lot of trip-ups, but after another few months, the recovery scores on my health tracker started to improve and I began to feel better. I could handle more stress again without falling into a pit of nausea.

I took the next nursing contract, one that demanded sixteen-hour shifts with a large serving of stress. And it was fine. I mean, it wasn't the most fun I've ever had, but it was fine. I was fine.

I have experienced only a few, exponentially milder anxiety attacks since.

Of course, not having an attack isn't the point. As you've learned, we're not here to stop hard times, but to increase our ability to weather them and prevent them from getting worse. That's the win.

Whether we're in the thick of it or enjoying life, there is work to be done. Work that increases our freedom to live a big life. If we're really lucky, that work might not only help us, but also elicit curiosity and encourage preparedness in others.

HIGH AGENCY HUMAN

The mission of *High Agency Human* is simple: to provide you with the freedom to live big, no matter what life throws your way. This state is achievable with increased personal agency and preparedness, which you can develop through the concepts and actions shared in the pages you've just read. Start from where you are, as you are, applying whatever resonates or aligns best with your goals. Apply a reduction if one area of life is a bit much at the moment, or boost your protective buffers to really get ahead if you're doing well overall.

Brandon, the shooting survivor turned charity CEO, decided that he wanted and needed to take on another big challenge. He ran a half, then a full marathon after recovery and both felt great to accomplish. Instead of waiting for the next hurdle, Brandon chose one: completing a full Ironman, something he'd never done before. When I asked how he managed to fit the intense training regimen into his life, he messaged back saying, "I am hermiting right now until [the event in] August, that's my strategy."

This is reduction in action, and you now understand that this strategy, building protective buffers, pursing peak conditioning, and establishing preparedness aren't emergency responses, they're a proactive approach to life. You've learned that high agency isn't a trait, but a practice. And you now have a playbook to navigate hard times with grit instead of reactivity and guesswork.

You're running the show. Not adversity. You.

And you should run it, because how else are you going to live big? How else will you make the best of the time you have? In *Journey to Ixtlan*, Carlos Castaneda writes, "There is one simple thing wrong with you—you think you have plenty of time… If you don't think your life is going to last forever, what are you waiting for? Why the hesitation to change?"

We all have an unknown expiration date, and while our time is ours to do with as we see fit, the thought that keeps me on track is: *Do I want to waste it or seize it?*

Seize it. Of course. I can't stomach the thought of wasting it, that would be selfish—a perspective best expressed through the response I gave when asked what I would like people to think about on Remembrance Day: The best way we can honor those who died overseas is to live our best lives and take in experiences with a grateful heart. It is our duty to do our best to live the life they never had the chance to fulfill.

It is our responsibility to live our best life. This level of agency and ownership is what I have talked about throughout this book, so instead of taking my foot off the gas after experiencing anxiety attacks, I focused on replenishing protective buffers, mastering the mundane, and pursuing peak conditioning. This was all to achieve and then maintain a strong base for the next hurdle, which may be health-related or something different altogether.

Continue to live big. After all, as Thoreau wrote, "Wealth is the ability to fully experience life." I think Matt would've smiled at the way I got off the floor and back to living a courageous, adventurous life.

It's hard to write what a big life looks like for me; I keep no bucket list of events and must-visit locations tucked away. Instead, my ideal is to increase both my ability to weather storms and my freedom to fully immerse in moments that provide that high of aliveness we all love so much. This will likely mean more trips to the polar regions to feel small yet connected, side quests to new countries with friends, and whatever large, unexpected hurdles come my way next.

As for Ron, he is no longer a scrappy teenager in the woods with mismatched preparedness gear or the new conservation officer experiencing wildfires for the first time. Ron is now a decorated, well-respected military veteran and seasoned conservation officer working in northern BC. His preparedness has gone beyond a first aid kit in the truck and a checklist for evacuations, and he regularly searches for and tests new emergency equipment for work. He strives for the best for his coworkers and community, always. His adventures and stories are ones that have us all listening for hours, captivated, around a bonfire. He's living his dream job and his big life, and he excels in both.

Brandon completed his first-ever Ironman, one he originally aimed to finish in under eleven hours. A flat tire happened not once, but twice during the cycle portion of the race and he had to adjust his expectations. The new plan was simply to finish and have fun along the way. He did just that. Brandon's big life includes setting lofty goals, ones that force him to stretch. Next, he aims to complete a full Ironman in under ten hours and thirty minutes and bring his business to a very healthy six-figure income benchmark. His charity, Hit the Ground Running, continues to help other shooting survivors with treatments and therapies.

The tools and perspective you've gained here are more than strategies to withstand adversity; they are openings into possibility. We have different paths and different outcomes, but each of us are all in. The path might not be immersing oneself writing and travel like me, completing an Ironman like Brandon, or working as a conservation officer like Ron. But it's something. Something you can create, build, and experience with that extra space, that extra breathing room, that extra time. With preparation, awareness, and agency at your back, your courage can flow freely.

It's your turn to live big. This your invitation not just to endure, but expand. Start today, right now, even. Take one chapter, one small section of this book to work on. Then the next, and the next.

And when the seemingly constant barrage of chaos threatens to overwhelm or an unexpected adversity knocks at your door, stand steady. The work to withstand has been done.

BOOK CLUB

Discussion Questions

---

1. What does "agency" mean to you now, after reading this book? How has your definition shifted from the beginning to the end?

2. Agency is a range. It is often described as a muscle that needs to be exercised. Where in your life are you training it well? Where is it atrophying?

3. The book introduces protective buffers as practical ways to brace for adversity. Which buffer do you need to strengthen most?

4. How does the concept of mastering the mundane apply to your daily routines? What small actions could you take to further build resilience?

5. The concept of moral arcs challenges readers to define their values before chaos hits. Consider your moral arcs: How might you act on them in a future high-stress moment?

6. Which story or metaphor stuck with you most? Why do you think it resonated with you?

7. This book reframes adversity as inevitable, not avoidable. How has that mindset shift impacted how you see your past and approach your future?

8. What does it mean to you to "live a big life"? Are you already living it, or do you have a plan to shift toward it?

BIG LIFE

Reflective Questions

---

1. What do my recent actions say my priorities are?

2. What do my recent thoughts say my priorities are?

3. What actions did I take a year ago to get me where I am today?

4. What actions do I need to take to reach my goals a year from now?

5. What traits and skills are a consistent through-line in my successes so far?

6. What habits and perceptions are a consistent through-line in my challenges so far?

7. What would the much older version of me want me to enjoy right now?

8. What would the much older version of me want me to prepare for right now?

9. If my best, healthier years are right now, what should I be spending them doing?

10. If my best, healthier years are right now, who should I be spending them with?

Next Steps

Subscribe to the Big Life Newsletter
at vickiemlanthier.com.

Find additional book resources,
and take the high agency quiz,
at highagencyhuman.com.

ACKNOWLEDGMENTS

WHEN I STARTED WRITING THIS book, it wasn't this book at all. It was a collection of stories and thoughts with no defined or helpful road for the reader. I was simply getting it all out. The second iteration of this book was a full manuscript that felt, well, boring. Which brings us to this version, the melding of writing as a craft, what I feel in my bones, and how it can serve the reader. I would still be writing stories just for me if I hadn't happened upon editor AJ Harper, her team, and the incredible community of writers they've created.

Thank you, Zoë Bird, Choi Messer, and KellyAnn Bessa, for your expert edits and patience as I worked through them. Pete Garceau, I lucked out when you said yes to designing the cover. Thank you for the much-loved design and for sharing your own high agency stories with me.

Thank you, North American Rescue; strength and conditioning coach Kevin Toonen; and author Dan Pronk, who read and shared an article I wrote about my first mass casualty incident. You made me realize that I had something worth sharing with the world.

The biggest of thanks to Ron Leblanc, Brandon Peacock, and Christian Schauf for trusting me with your stories and sharing your valuable insights with readers. Thank you, Dr.

D.J. Cook, for taking the time to explain different aspects of neurology and bounce big ideas around with me.

Leslie, Jimmy, Mike, and Ted: Your fortitude and friendship are everything.

Most of all, thank you to friends and family who are likely tired of hearing me talk about writing and the topics in this book, yet forever support my endeavors with enthusiasm.

NOTES

CHAPTER 1: ADVERSITY ISN'T RUNNING THE SHOW

Robert Frost, "A Servant to Servants," *North of Boston* (New York, NY: Henry Holt and Company, 1915).

Albert Bandura, "Social Cognitive Theory: An Agentic Perspective," *Annual Review of Psychology* 52 (1): 1, 2001, doi.org/10.1146/annurev.psych.52.1.1, accessed November 4, 2025.

Albert Bandura, "Toward a Psychology of Human Agency," *Perspectives on Psychological Science* 1 (2): 164–80, 2006, doi.org/10.1111/j.1745-6916.2006.00011.x, accessed November 4, 2025.

Shaun Gallagher, "Philosophical Conceptions of the Self: Implications for Cognitive Science," *Trends in Cognitive Sciences* 4 (1): 14–21, January 1, 2000, doi.org/10.1016/S1364-6613(99)01417-5, accessed November 4, 2025.

Patrick Haggard, "Sense of Agency in the Human Brain," *Nature Reviews Neuroscience* 18: 196–207, March 2, 2017, doi.org/10.1038/nrn.2017.14, accessed November 4, 2025.

American Psychological Association, "The Road to Resilience," 2020, apa.org/topics/resilience, accessed November 4, 2025.

Richard G. Tedeschi and Lawrence G. Calhoun, "Posttraumatic Growth: Conceptual Foundations and Empirical Evidence," *Psychological Inquiry* 15 (1): 1–18, November 19, 2009, doi.org/10.1207/s15327965pli1501_01, accessed November 4, 2025.

Brené Brown, *Daring Greatly: How the Courage to Be Vulnerable Transforms the Way We Live, Love, Parent, and Lead* (New York, NY: Gotham Books, 2012).

CHAPTER 2: PULL THE EMERGENCY BRAKE

Martin Gilbert, *Winston S. Churchill: Challenge of War 1914-1916* (Hillsdale, MI: Hillsdale College Press, 1971).

C. Benjet, E. Bromet, E.G. Karam, et al, "The epidemiology of traumatic event exposure worldwide: results from the World Mental Health Survey Consortium," *Psychological Medicine* 46 (2): 327-43, October 29, 2015, doi.org/10.1017/S0033291715001981, accessed November 4, 2025.

USAFacts, "Charted: The History of U.S. Recessions," Visual Capitalist, August 1, 2025, voronoiapp.com/economy/A-History-of-American-Recessions-6053, accessed November 4, 2025.

Marco Del Giudice, Bruce J. Ellis, and Elizabeth A. Shirtcliff, "The Adaptive Calibration Model of Stress Responsivity," *Development and Psychopathology* 23 (4): 1007–27, 2011, doi:10.1016/j.neubiorev.2010.11.007, accessed November 4, 2025.

Hengchen Dai, Katherine L. Milkman, and Jason Riis, "The Fresh Start Effect: Temporal Landmarks Motivate Aspirational Behavior," *Management Science* 60 (10): 2563–82, 2014. doi.org/10.1287/mnsc.2014.1901, accessed November 4, 2025.

Leidy Klotz, *Subtract: The Untapped Science of Less* (New York, NY: Flatiron Books, 2021).

Abraham H. Maslow, "A Theory of Human Motivation," *Psychological Review* 50 (4): 370–96, 1943, doi.org/10.1037/h0054346, accessed November 4, 2025.

Ann S. Masten, "Ordinary Magic: Resilience Processes in Development," *American Psychologist* 56 (3): 227–38, 2001, doi.org/10.1037/0003-066X.56.3.227, accessed November 4, 2025.

Gabor Maté, *When the Body Says No: Exploring the Stress-Disease Connection* (Toronto, ON: John Wiley & Sons, 2003).

Greg McKeown, *Essentialism: The Disciplined Pursuit of Less* (New York, NY: Crown Business, 2014).

Marie Forleo, *Everything Is Figureoutable* (New York, NY: Portfolio/Penguin, 2019).

CHAPTER 3: CALIBRATE YOUR BASELINE

George A. Bonanno, "Loss, Trauma, and Human Resilience: Have We Underestimated the Human Capacity to Thrive After Extremely Aversive Events?" *American Psychologist* 59

(1): 20–28, 2004, doi.org/10.1037/0003-066X.59.1.20, accessed November 4, 2025.

Alia J. Crum, Peter Salovey, and Shawn Achor, "Rethinking Stress: The Role of Mindsets in Determining the Stress Response," *Journal of Health Psychology* 18 (6): 731–38, 2013, doi.org/10.1177/1359105312459091, accessed November 4, 2025.

Brad Stulberg, *Master of Change* (New York, NY: HarperOne, 2023).

James Clear, *Atomic Habits* (New York, NY: Avery Publishing, 2018).

Robert Croak and Austin Hankwitz, *Rich Habits* podcast, richhabitspodcast.com/, accessed November 4, 2025.

Michael O'Brien, *The Rich Roll Podcast,* richroll.com/podcast/michael-obrien-824, 2024, accessed November 4, 2025.

John LaRosa, "Self-Improvement Market Recovers from the Pandemic, Worth $13.4 Billion in the U.S.," Market Research Blog, September 8, 2023, blog.marketresearch.com/self-improvement-market-recovers-from-the-pandemic-worth-13.4-billion-in-the-u.s, accessed November 4, 2025.

Federal Emergency Management Agency (FEMA), "Disaster Declarations Summary," 2023, fema.gov/about/reports-and-data/openfema , accessed November 4, 2025.

Viktor E. Frankl, *Man's Search for Meaning* (Boston, MA: Beacon Press, 1946).

Dean G. Kilpatrick, Heidi S. Resnick, Melissa E. Milanak, et al, "National Estimates of Exposure to Traumatic Events and PTSD Prevalence Using DSM-IV and DSM-5 Criteria," *Journal of Traumatic Stress* 26 (5): 537–47, October 22, 2013, doi.org/10.1002/jts.21848, accessed November 4, 2025.

Friedrich Nietzsche (translated by H. B. Nisbet), *On the Genealogy of Morality: A Polemic*, (Cambridge, MA: Cambridge University Press, 1887).

Mark D. Seery, E. Alison Holman, and Roxane Cohen Silver, "Whatever Does Not Kill Us: Cumulative Lifetime Adversity, Vulnerability, and Resilience," *Journal of Personality and Social Psychology* 99 (6): 1025–44, 2010, doi.org/10.1037/a0021344, accessed November 4, 2025.

Peter Sterling and Joseph Eyer, "Allostasis: A New Paradigm to Explain Arousal Pathways," *In Handbook of Life Stress, Cognition, and Health*, edited by S. Fisher and J. Reason, 629–49 (New York, NY: John Wiley & Sons, 1988).

CHAPTER 4: MASTER THE MUNDANE

C. S. Lewis, *Mere Christianity: A Revised and Amplified Edition, with a New Introduction, of the Three Books Broadcast Talks, Christian Behaviour, and Beyond Personality* (New York, NY: HarperOne, 2009).

George Vecsey, "With Wooden as Teacher, The First Lesson Was Shoelaces," *New York Times*, June 4, 2010, nytimes.com/2010/06/05/sports/ncaabasketball/05wizard.html, accessed November 4, 2025.

HIGH AGENCY HUMAN

Robert Greene interview by Dr. Michael Gervais, episode 497, *Finding Mastery* podcast, 2019, findingmastery.com/podcasts/robert-greene-2/, accessed November 4, 2025.

Miyamoto Musashi (translated by Thomas F. Cleary, *The Book of Five Rings* (Boston, MA: Shambhala, 2005).

"Warren Buffett," Forbes, forbes.com/profile/warren-buffett/, accessed November 4, 2025.

Mike Horn Facebook post, August 5, 2025, Facebook.com/share/v/16UJ42viDe/, accessed November 4, 2025.

Y.E. Willems, N. Boesen, J. Li, C. Finkenauer, and M. Bartels, The heritability of self-control: A meta-analysis. *Neuroscience Biobehavior Review*, 100: 324-334, May 2019, doi: 10.1016/j.neubiorev.2019.02.012. Epub Feb 26, 2019, PMID: 30822436, accessed November 4, 2025.

Leila Hormozi Instagram post, January 31, 2024, instagram.com/reel/C2yeF3TAYPP/, accessed November 4, 2025.

Randall Hyde, "Ubiquity: The Fallacy of Premature Optimization," ACM, February 2009, ubiquity.acm.org/article.cfm?id=1513451, accessed November 4, 2025.

Mike Michalowicz, *Profit First: Transform Your Business from a Cash-Eating Monster to a Money-Making Machine* (New York, NY: Portfolio/Penguin, 2017).

Brad Stulberg, "Protocols and Peak Performance," *The Growth Equation*, July 16, 2024, thegrowtheq.com/protocols-and-peak-performance/, accessed November 4, 2025.

Interview with Dr. Uma Naidoo, episode 840, "How Nutrition Fuels Mental Health," *The Rich Roll Podcast*, richroll.com/podcast/uma-naidoo-840/, accessed November 4, 2025.

Jean-Philippe Chaput, Julie Carrier, Célyne Bastien, Geneviève Gariépy, and Ian Janssen, "Economic Burden of Insufficient Sleep Duration in Canadian Adults," *Sleep Health* 8, no. 3 (June 2022): 298–302, doi.org/10.1016/j.sleh.2022.02.001, accessed November 4, 2025.

CDC Sleep, "FastStats: Sleep in Adults," Centers for Disease Control and Prevention, May 15, 2024, cdc.gov/sleep/data-research/facts-stats/adults-sleep-facts-and-stats.html, accessed November 4, 2025.

Shingo Kitamura, Yasuko Katayose, Kyoko Nakazaki, Yuki Motomura, Kentaro Oba, Ruri Katsunuma, Yuri Terasawa, et al, "Estimating Individual Optimal Sleep Duration and Potential Sleep Debt." *Scientific Reports* 6, no. 1, October 24, 2016, doi.org/10.1038/srep35812, accessed November 4, 2025.

Edward J. Howden, Shireen Sarma, Justin S. Lawley, et al, "Reversing the Cardiac Effects of Sedentary Aging in Middle Age—A Randomized Controlled Trial," *Circulation* 137 (15): 1549–60, January 8, 2018, doi.org/10.1161/circulationaha.117.030617, accessed November 4, 2025.

Fuzhong Wang, Yiqiang Gao, Zhiwei Han, et al, "A Systematic Review and Meta-Analysis of 90 Cohort Studies of Social Isolation, Loneliness and Mortality," *Nature Human Behaviour* 7: 1307–19, June 19, 2023, doi.org/10.1038/s41562-023-01617-6, accessed November 4, 2025.

CHAPTER 5: ACTIVATE HIGH AGENCY

Jean-Paul Sartre, *Existentialism and Human Emotions* (Secaucus, NJ: Carol Publishing Group, 1999).

Franklin D. Roosevelt, "Fireside Chat," The American Presidency Project, September 11, 1941, presidency.ucsb.edu/documents/fireside-chat-11, accessed November 4, 2025.

Daniel Goleman, *Emotional Intelligence: Why It Can Matter More than IQ* (New York, NY: Bantam, 1995).

Ryan Holiday, *Courage Is Calling* (New York, NY: Penguin Random House, 2021).

A. H. Jaffri and S. Saliba, "Does Verbal Encouragement Change Dynamic Balance? The Effect of Verbal Encouragement on Star Excursion Balance Test Performance in Chronic Ankle Instability," *Brazilian Journal of Physical Therapy* 25 (5): 617–22, September–October 2021, doi.org/10.1016/j.bjpt.2021.04.002, accessed November 4, 2025.

Jon Kabat-Zinn, "Overwhelm," *Journal of Mindfulness* 10 (2): 50–58, 2019.

Plato (translated by C. D. C. Reeve), *The Republic* (Indianapolis, IN: Hackett, 2007).

Anja Ritter, Matthias Franz, Wolfgang H. R. Miltner, and Thomas Weiss, "How Words Impact on Pain," *Brain and Behavior* 9 (9): e01377, August 1, 2019, doi.org/10.1002/brb3.1377, accessed November 4, 2025.

Jocko Willink and Leif Babin, *Extreme Ownership: How U.S. Navy SEALs Lead and Win* (New York, NY: St. Martin's Press, 2015).

CHAPTER 6: BOOST PROTECTIVE BUFFERS

Nassim Nicholas Taleb, *The Black Swan: The Impact of the Highly Improbable* (New York, NY: Random House, 2010).

Natural Resources Canada, "Earthquakes in Southwestern British Columbia," earthquakescanada.nrcan.gc.ca/pprs-pprp/pubs/GF-GI/GEOFACT_earthquakes-SW-BC_e.pdf, accessed November 4, 2025.

Michael Easter, *The Comfort Crisis: Embrace Discomfort to Reclaim Your Wild, Happy, Healthy Self* (New York, NY: Rodale Books, 2021).

American Psychological Association, "Stress in America™: 2023 Top-Line Results," November 2023, apa.org/news/press/releases/stress/2023/collective-trauma-recovery, accessed November 4, 2025.

Bankrate, "The State of Emergency Savings in America," June 26, 2025, bankrate.com/banking/savings/emergency-savings-report, accessed November 4, 2025.

U.S. Department of Health and Human Services, "Advisory on the Healing Effects of Social Connection and Community," Office of the U.S. Surgeon General, 2023, hhs.gov/surgeongeneral/reports-and-publications/connection/index.html, accessed November 4, 2025.

HIGH AGENCY HUMAN

CHAPTER 7: PURSUE PEAK CONDITIONING

Morihei Ueshiba and John Stevens, *The Art of Peace* (Boulder, CO: Shambhala, 2023).

Teena Apeles, "Steve Nash on the Qualities of a Natural Leader," AskMen, April 19, 2012, askmen.com/sports/news/steve-nash-interview-2.html, accessed November 4, 2025.

Nicolette Sowder, Wilder Child Nature-Connected Parenting, wilderchild.com, accessed November 4, 2025.

Alia J. Crum, Peter Salovey, and Shawn Achor, "Rethinking Stress: The Role of Mindsets in Determining the Stress Response," *Journal of Personality and Social Psychology* 104, no. 4, 716–33, April 2013, doi.org/10.1037/a0031201, accessed November 4, 2025.

Harvard University, "DSM Recognizes Moral Injury, Thanks to Human Flourishing Program Research," The Institute for Quantitative Social Science, September 11, 2025, iq.harvard.edu/news/2025/09/dsm-recognizes-moral-injury-thanks-human-flourishing-program-research, accessed November 4, 2025.

Brett T. Litz, Nathan Stein, Eileen Delaney, et al, "Moral Injury and Moral Repair in War Veterans: A Preliminary Model and Intervention Strategy," *Clinical Psychology Review* 29 (8): 695–706, 2009.

Bruce D. Perry and Oprah Winfrey, *What Happened to You? Conversations on Trauma, Resilience, and Healing* (New York, NY: Flatiron Books, 2021).

CHAPTER 8: SWITCH OFF AUTOPILOT

Marcus Aurelius, *Meditations* (New York, NY: Random House, 2002).

Peter Attia, *Outlive: The Science and Art of Longevity* (New York, NY: Harmony Books, 2013).

Norman Doidge, *The Brain That Changes Itself* (New York, NY: Viking, 2007).

CHAPTER 9: HIGH AGENCY HUMAN

Joseph Campbell, *Pathways to Bliss: Mythology and Personal Transformation* (Novato, CA: New World Library, 2004).

Carlos Castaneda, *Journey to Ixtlan* (New York: Simon & Schuster, 1972).

Henry David Thoreau, *Walden* (Boston, MA: Ticknor and Fields, 1854).

ABOUT THE AUTHOR

 VICKIE LANTHIER IS AN AUTHOR who shares insights into increasing personal agency and weathering adversity. Drawing on her military career, four deployments, and adventures in entrepreneurship, she delivers strategies that help readers work through hardships and challenges.

Vickie worked at National Defence (Canada) for twenty-six years, serving in the military and later as a consultant. She then founded girlgonegood.com, a values-based website that provides hiking resources and has donated over $27,000 to local charities. In 2020, she completed a bachelor of science in nursing honors program at the University of Ottawa and became a registered nurse.

Vickie speaks on experiencing mass casualty incidents and believes in living a big life, no matter what adversity is thrown our way. She currently lives in Perth, Ontario—not Australia, though she wouldn't say no to living there too. Connect with her at vickiemlanthier.com.

www.ingramcontent.com/pod-product-compliance
Lightning Source LLC
LaVergne TN
LVHW041944070526
838199LV00051BA/2893